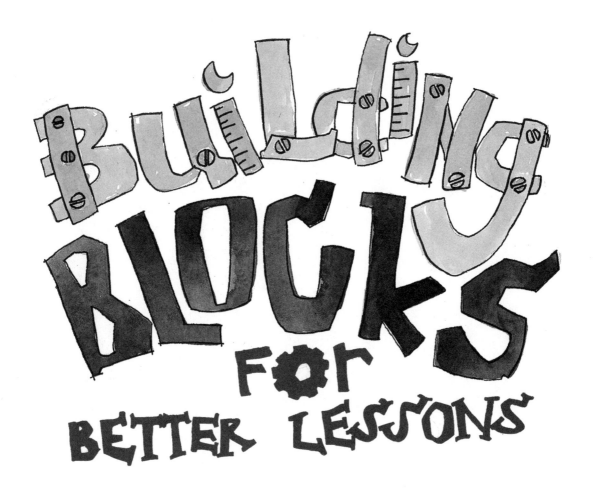

# Beth Lefgren
# Jennifer Jackson

Bookcraft
Salt Lake City, Utah

Library of Congress Catalog Card Number 98-72873
ISBN 1-57008-528-5


First Printing, 1998


Printed in the United States of America

# Contents

# Preface

This book was written with you in mind! No matter what teaching situation you find yourself in—family, church, Scouting, or community—here you will find activities and ideas to meet your varied needs.

The purpose of this book is to give you a wide variety of activities and ideas that will enrich your lessons. These ideas have been designed to strengthen, clarify, and make your lessons more memorable. You will discover that they are easy to use, with basic materials and minimal preparation required.

We hope that you will feel this book has reached its goal by offering you a wide range of resources. Games, stories, object lessons, hands-on activities, scripture references, and music selections are only the beginning of what you will find.

*Building Blocks for Better Lessons* will be a valuable resource to make your lessons easier, more interesting, and more successful. You will truly experience the joy of teaching as you watch your students understand and apply your lessons in their lives. We are appreciative of the opportunity to assist you in this important work.

# How to Use This Book

You will find that this book contains a wide variety of resources to enrich and strengthen your lessons. We have endeavored to offer a large selection of topics to meet your varied needs. To assist you in the use of these ideas, the following may be helpful:

1. Notice that the topics are arranged in alphabetical order for ease of browsing and locating. Many subjects can be interchanged. For example, an activity on activation might easily be used for the subject of family. You will discover the possibilities are limitless as you use your personal creativity and inspiration.
2. Each topic contains many activities and ideas. These have been designed to *supplement* your lesson. Prayerfully select only those ideas that will strengthen your lesson objective. Consider age group, time allowance, and other special needs as you select your material. Remember, more is not always better.
3. The activities have been created to enhance class participation. Your greatest resources are your students. Try to involve as many as possible in the activities. The lessons will become more meaningful and memorable as they take an active role.
4. A variety of object lessons are included in the book. Practice them before your lesson. This will allow you to give a smooth presentation. Also included are short stories, parables, and analogies. If possible, display pictures or objects as the stories are related. Visual aids will increase the attention of your group.
5. Suggested songs are from the *Children's Songbook,* published in 1989, and *Hymns,* 1985. A section on using music in your lesson can be found on page 86.
6. Scripture stories can teach many lessons in a powerful way. Prayerfully select those that will reinforce the objective of your lesson. Additional ideas for using scriptures in your lessons are included on page 85.

We know as you apply these guidelines you will experience wonderful success.

# ENRICHMENT
# TOOLS

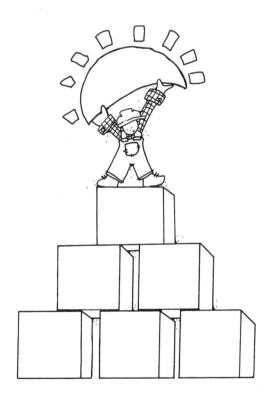

# Activation

*Choose one or more of the following ideas to enrich your lesson.*

## Activity: "Activation Starts with the Golden Rule"

### Preparation:

Print the following situations on the chalkboard.
1. You just moved into a new home.
2. A member of your family is seriously ill.
3. You are painting your home.
4. You are trying to carry a big box.
5. You see someone you know in the store.

### Application:

Review the situations written on the chalkboard. Explain that the class must think about the circumstances as if they were happening to them and tell what they hope someone else would do for them in the same case.

Have your class turn to Doctrine and Covenants 38:24 and read it aloud together. Talk about the word *esteem*. Help your class understand that we should treat others the same way we would like to be treated. When we do this, we help other people understand what the Savior is like, and when they understand how much the Savior loves them they will want to be part of his church.

## Activity: "Friendship Prepares Others for the Gospel"

### Materials Needed:

Small balloons

### Application:

Pass the small balloons out to class members. Ask them if they have ever tried to blow up a small, stiff balloon. Have them try to blow up the balloons. Now show them how a balloon can be stretched to allow it to be more flexible.

Liken this to working with nonmembers or inactive members. Trying to convert or reactivate them can be a difficult task because many feel very uncomfortable about the gospel. As we show them our love, through friendship and example, they become more open and flexible about listening to the truth and receiving gospel instruction.

Have class members stretch and work with the balloons for about a minute before they try to blow up the balloons again. Talk about how much easier it was to blow up the balloons when they were more flexible.

## Activity: "Sharing the Light"

*(This is an outdoors activity.)*

### Materials Needed:

Votive candles for everyone in your group, jar lids, and matches.

### Application:

Place a candle on the inside of a jar lid (this works well to catch wax). Give a candle to each person. Do this activity outside and designate a starting and finishing line. Explain that the purpose is for everyone to make it to the finishing line with their candles still lit. Tell them that they will need to work together to accomplish this goal. If someone's candle goes out they will need to relight it using their own candle. The object is to work together and help each other get there.

Light everyone's candle at the starting line. Give them verbal encouragement as they go. When everyone has successfully made it to the finish line sit together as a group and compare this to sharing the gospel. Help them to understand that our goal in life is to return to Heavenly Father, but to do this we must help others along the way by sharing the light of the gospel. It is our responsibility to help others to return to Heavenly Father also. Discuss the importance of being a missionary every day of our lives.

## Object Lesson: "Activation Begins with Friendship"

### Materials Needed:

Two pots, dirt, two carrots with greens, and a hand spade.

### Preparation:

"Plant" a carrot in each pot, with greens exposed. Make sure that the dirt in each pot is *firmly* packed around the carrot.

### Application:

Show the two potted carrots to the class. Liken each carrot to an inactive or nonmember person. Have a class member come up and yank on the greens of one carrot to remove it. The greens will come up but this should leave the carrot in the pot. Explain that when we try to pull, push, or force someone into activity, we are usually unsuccessful.

Now focus on the other potted carrot. Begin to work the soil with the hand spade. Tell the class that when we loosen the soil around the carrot it will be easier to lift the carrot out. Remind the class that care must be taken not to bruise or damage the carrot during the process. Then lift the carrot out of the dirt. Talk about activation—why it is important to do it correctly and for the right reasons. Discuss ways that we can prepare the inactive for activation; you could liken the spade to unconditional love.

## Additional Enrichment:

### *Hymns:*

- "Dear to the Heart of the Shepherd," *Hymns,* no. 221.
- "Each Life That Touches Ours for Good," *Hymns,* no. 293.
- "Help Me Teach with Inspiration," *Hymns,* no. 281.
- "The Things I Do," *Children's Songbook,* pp. 170–71.

### *Scripture Stories:*

- The shepherd finds the lost sheep (see Luke 15:3–7).
- King Limhi's people are welcomed by King Mosiah (see Mosiah 22:11–14).
- The Nephites agree to protect the Anti-Nephi-Lehites (see Alma 27:21–27).

# Adversity

---

*Choose one or more of the following ideas to enrich your lesson.*

## Activity: "Blessings Follow Adversity"

### Materials Needed:

Six pictures: *The Crossing of the Red Sea* (62100), *Daniel in the Lions' Den* (62096), *Stilling the Storm* (62139), *The Prodigal Son* (62155), *Lehi and His People Arrive in the Promised Land* (62045), *Miracle of the Sea Gulls* (62603), or others of your own choosing.

### Preparation:

Mount the six pictures on a wall or display area in your classroom. Cover each picture with a plain piece of paper.

### Application:

Briefly discuss how adversity can help us be more aware of our many blessings. Tell your class that each picture depicts a story from the scriptures. Explain that as these people went through their trials they received many blessings from the Lord. Uncover one picture and talk about the adversity experienced in the story, how the Lord blessed the people in the face of their adversities, and how they showed their gratitude in return. (For example: The Children of Israel were slaves in Egypt for many years. The Lord blessed them by opening the Red Sea, allowing them to escape Pharaoh's army. They sang songs of praise to Heavenly Father.)

## Analogy: "The Pearl"

The clear water flows down the river, slowly moving past the colony of mussels attached to rocks near the shore. Although unable to move on its own, each mussel feeds upon the microorganisms that float by, and occasionally a particle of sand becomes lodged in the mussel's sensitive tissue, causing great irritation.

Because the mussel is unable to expel the sand, it begins to cover it with a layer of nacre, or mother-of-pearl. Over the months and years the little mussel continues to cover that irritation with layer after layer of mother-of-pearl until that grain of sand becomes a pearl—a gem that many prize for its beauty.

Adversity usually causes some kind of disruption in our lives, which in turn can lead to little things that become irritating to ourselves and others. As we strive to allow the characteristics of patience and love to work within us we can, like the mussel, allow adversity to make something beautiful within us.

## Object Lesson: "Testimony Helps Us Deal with Adversity"

### Materials Needed:

Two paper lunch sacks and four lemons

### Preparation:

Carefully unseal half of the bottom seam on one paper bag.

### Application:

Have two class members stand at the front of the room. Give each one a bag. Explain that the unsealed sack is like a person without a strong testimony. Tell them that the lemons represent the adversity that everyone experiences in life. Drop two lemons into the sack that has a partially sealed bottom, pointing out that when our testimonies are not strong we are not able to deal effectively with adversity.

Contrast this by dropping two lemons into the other sack and likening it to a person with a steadfast testimony. If you desire, close the top of the bag and shake vigorously. Point out that those with a strong testimony can cope with a great deal of adversity.

## Story: "Joseph F. Smith Receives Comfort Through a Revelation"

Much of the love found in President Joseph F. Smith's family came from the perfect example of devotion and caring that their husband and father constantly showed. Few fathers showed greater love for wives and children or were more earnestly concerned for their welfare than President Smith.

Ten times, Joseph F. Smith and his wives passed through the sorrow that came with the loss of a beloved child. Although each loss was painful, the 1918 death of his eldest son, the Apostle Hyrum M. Smith, was particularly difficult to the aging prophet. As in times past, Joseph F. Smith turned to the Lord for comfort through prayer, meditation, and scripture study.

Eight months later, the day before October conference, a glorious revelation that dealt with the redemption of the dead was given to President Smith. With great humility he declared ". . . I dare not, attempt to enter upon many things that are resting upon my mind this morning . . . I have not lived alone these five months. I have dwelt in the spirit of prayer, of supplication, of faith and of determination; and I have had my communication with the Spirit of the Lord continuously. . . ." (In Conference Report, October 1918, p. 2.)

## Additional Enrichment:

### Hymns:

- "Count Your Blessings," *Hymns,* no. 241.
- "Nearer, My God, to Thee," *Hymns,* no. 100.
- "Where Can I Turn for Peace," *Hymns,* no. 129.

### *Scripture Stories:*

- Joseph is falsely accused (see Genesis 39).
- Paul casts out an evil spirit and is thrown in prison (see Acts 16:16–40).
- Limhi's people turn to Heavenly Father (see Mosiah 21).
- Joseph Smith receives comfort in Liberty Jail (see Doctrine and Covenants 121).

# Agency

*Choose one or more of the following ideas to enrich your lesson.*

## Activity: "Agency Has Consequences"

### *Preparation:*

On one side of a chalkboard, list the following actions: stay up too late, exercise, arrive late for school or work, break a traffic law, smile, eat too much, drive on a flat tire, prepare well for an assignment or test. If you desire, list any others that are applicable for your class. Draw a line down the middle of the chalkboard.

### *Application:*

Briefly discuss what the word *consequences* means. Tell your class that every choice has a consequence. Sometimes the consequences do not happen for a long time, but there is always a consequence. Go through the list of actions and have class members tell what the consequence of each action might be. Determine whether the action shows obedience or disobedience. On the other side of the line, write one or two consequences of each action. If time permits, talk about consequences that might occur for other actions.

## Activity: "Game of Choices"

### *Materials Needed:*

White typing paper (enough to make a path from one side of cultural hall to the other), 12 to 16 pieces of blue paper, 12 to 16 paper cups, spinner or one die.

### *Preparation:*

Make a list of positive and negative choices, including their "consequences." For example:

1. Read scriptures for one month (go forward two squares)
2. Too busy to pray (go back three squares)
3. Visit a sick neighbor (go forward one square)
4. Make cookies but don't deliver them (stay in place)

Make 12 to 16 copies of the choices list. Cut into strips so that one of the choices is on each slip. Place one complete set in each paper cup.

Set up the game area by arranging the white paper in a path from one side of the cultural hall to the other. At various intervals, replace 12 to 16 white squares with a square made from blue paper. Place a cup of choices next to each blue square.

### *Application:*

Have one person use the spinner to determine how many steps forward can be taken. Have each class member repeat that process. Continue to spin until everyone has reached the end. As a person lands on a blue square, he or she must choose from the choice cup and follow the directions.

Explain that this game can be like life. It is filled with choices; some are good while others are bad. Help your class understand that in real life we do not draw for our choices but the choices we make influence our path toward Heavenly Father.

## Object Lesson: "Understanding Agency"

### *Materials Needed:*

Make enough sugar cookies for every class member to have two. Have enough frosting for half of the cookies.

### *Preparation:*

Ice half of the cookies and arrange on plate.
Place the other half of the cookies on a plate and cover.

### *Application:*

Take the plain cookie plate around the class and insist that each class member take a cookie. Tell your class that some choices are better than others and briefly discuss why it is important to make good choices. Tell them that you insisted on the plain cookie because it is a good choice. Explain that it may not taste as good as the iced cookies but it is better for them.

Ask your class how they feel about having their choice made for them. Help them understand that this was similar to Satan's plan in the premortal life. Explain that he wanted to make all of the right choices for us. Heavenly Father knew that Satan's plan would not allow us to grow from our experiences—we would not become wise.

Pass the plate of iced cookies around and allow everyone the opportunity to exchange their cookies. Remind class members that they can now choose whichever cookie they want. When everyone has chosen let the class eat their cookies.

Explain that Heavenly Father knew we would make unwise choices and he provided a way that we could repent. Discuss the plan of happiness and how agency and consequences are an important part of that plan.

## Additional Enrichment:

### *Hymns:*

- "Choose the Right," *Hymns,* no. 239.
- "Dare to Do Right," Children's Songbook, p. 158.
- "Do What Is Right," *Hymns,* no. 237.
- "I Lived in Heaven," *Children's Songbook,* p. 4.

### *Scripture Story:*

- The war in the premortal existence was fought for agency (see Moses 4:1–3; Abraham 3:22–28).

# Attitude

*Choose one or more of the following ideas to enrich your lesson.*

## Activity: "I Shall Not Fear"

### Preparation:

Write 2 Timothy 1:7 ("For God hath not given us the spirit of fear; but of power, and of love, and of a sound mind.") at the top of the chalkboard.

Print the following scripture references only on separate slips of paper:

- 1 Samuel 17 (David and Goliath)
- Daniel 3 (Shadrach, Meshach, Abed-nego)
- Luke 8:22–25 (Christ calms the sea)
- 1 Nephi 16:18–32 (Nephi breaks his bow)
- Alma 57:19–27 (Helaman's stripling warriors fight in the war)

### Application:

Tell your class that we are all faced with situations that cause us to be afraid. Explain that it is normal to feel fear, but Heavenly Father has given us ways to overcome our fear and find our strength in him.

Pass the scripture references to class members. If you have a large class, divide them into groups for brainstorming. Answer the following questions for each scripture reference:

- Why were they afraid?
- How did they overcome their fear?
- How did Heavenly Father help them?

Help your class understand that Heavenly Father will help them too, but they must rely on him and not allow the spirit of fear to overcome them.

## Analogy: "The Dry Bone"

The dog vigilantly protected his bone, although it was dry and hard. Although it offered no real nourishment, it was regularly brought out and chewed upon—a favorite way to pass time. It offered hours and hours of chewing pleasure to the dog until eventually it did wear down. Soon after, it was replaced by another bone—equally dry and hard.

Like the dog's bone, anger is hard, dry, and without nourishment. Whenever we continue to gnaw upon the bones of misunderstanding, a habit grows until the harboring of a problem becomes a regular pastime. We can actually become so dependent on negative feelings that even when given an opportunity we would rather seek a replacement than a solution.

## Object Lesson: "Make Positive Attitudes a Habit"

### Materials Needed:

Sewing thread and two pencils

*Application:*

Ask a class member to assist you. Have him hold a pencil in each hand and wind the thread around the pencils once, leaving two to three inches of space between the pencils. Ask your assistant to break the thread. Now wind the thread around the pencils four or five times and have him try to break it. Ask if it was easier or harder.

Explain to the class that a positive attitude, like any habit, is developed by using it over and over, just like the thread was stronger after wrapping it over and over. Discuss various positive traits such as smiling, greeting others, cheerfulness, and so on.

## Object Lesson: "Negative Attitudes Can Be Destructive"

### *Materials Needed:*

A small container packed with moist sand, a 9″ x 13″ pan, and a glass of water.

### *Application:*

Tip the sand-packed container upside down in the pan. Carefully remove the container, leaving the packed sand in place. Ask your class what would happen if you poured water over the sand. Demonstrate by pouring a little of the glass of water over the packed sand. Explain that even a small amount of water begins to break down the sand. Show the class what happens when more water is poured over the sand.

Liken the water to negative attitudes. Even a little can be destructive to our lives. Help class members understand the importance of keeping negative attitudes out of our lives. Briefly discuss how this can be done.

## Object Lesson: "Repentance Helps Us Lose Negative Feelings"

### *Materials Needed:*

Paper, paintbrush, red water-base paint, black water-base paint, and a jar of water.

### *Application:*

Load the paintbrush with the red paint and make a letter "L" on the paper. Refresh the red paint, dip the tip of the paintbrush into the black paint and make a letter "I" after the "L". Without adding any more paint, paint the letter "F" at the end. Show the class how the little bit of black begins to take over the color of the letter.

Liken the black paint to negative feelings in our lives. Help the class understand that the longer we allow the negative feelings to stay, the stronger they become. Discuss ways to get rid of negative feelings. Explain that one way to overcome those feelings is through sincere repentance. When we repent of our negative feelings they are washed away and we are then able to focus on the blessings in our lives.

Demonstrate this idea by thoroughly rinsing the paintbrush in the jar of water. Load the brush with red paint and paint the letter "E" after the "F".

## Additional Enrichment:

### *Hymns:*

- "I Am Glad for Many Things," *Children's Songbook,* p. 151.
- "Scatter Sunshine," *Hymns,* no. 230.
- "School Thy Feelings," *Hymns,* no. 336.

### *Scripture Stories:*

- Moses sends twelve spies to Canaan (see Numbers 13; 14:1–9).
- Nephi breaks his bow (see 1 Nephi 16:18–32).

# Book of Mormon

*Choose one or more of the following ideas to enrich your lesson.*

## Activity: "The Book of Mormon—A Companion to the Bible"

### Materials Needed:

Two poster boards, marker, and tape.

### Preparation:

Write the last part of D&C 42:12 on one poster board: "Teach the principles of my gospel, which are in the Bible and the Book of Mormon, in the which is the fulness of the gospel." Cut the poster board with the verse on it into several pieces, similar to a jigsaw puzzle.

### Application:

Give members of your group some of the pieces of the scripture puzzle. (Reserve a few key pieces that would keep the class from being able to read the verse.) Invite those individuals with puzzle pieces to come up. Place the blank poster board on a table or other flat surface. Instruct them to put the puzzle together on the blank poster board. Tape the pieces down when they are done.

Display the poster with the unfinished puzzle on it. Ask the class if they can read the verse. They won't be able to because of the missing pieces. Tell them that like the puzzle, the Bible is missing some of the "plain and most precious" parts (see 1 Nephi 13:26) of the gospel. The Book of Mormon fills in some of those missing pieces and gives us the fulness of the gospel.

Use the missing pieces to complete the puzzle. Invite the group to read the scripture.

## Activity: "Hold to the Rod"

### Materials Needed:

A Book of Mormon, yarn, blindfold, and a piece of fruit for each person.

### Preparation:

Use the yarn to make a winding path in your room. Wrap it around chairs, tables, and so on.

### Application:

Explain to your group that each person will have an opportunity to be blindfolded and follow a path that will lead them to a reward. After securing their blindfolds, instruct class members to grasp the yarn and follow it. If they are careful and don't give up it will lead them to a reward. As they reach the finishing point take off their blindfolds and give them a piece of fruit. Repeat until each person has had a turn.

Read Lehi's vision of the "Tree of Life" as they eat their fruit (1 Nephi 8). Compare grasping and following the iron rod to your activity. Use the following questions to assist in your discussion:

What would have happened if you had let go of the yarn occasionally?

What would have happened if you got tired and gave up before reaching the end?

Did you feel self-conscious and worry about what others were thinking as they followed the path?

Explain that the iron rod is the word of God. We grasp and follow the iron rod by reading the Book of Mormon. If we read it and faithfully live by its precepts it will lead us back to Heavenly Father.

## Activity: "President Benson Speaks about the Book of Mormon"

### *Materials Needed:*

A copy of President Benson's conference address "The Book of Mormon—Keystone of Our Religion" (*Ensign,* November 1986, pp. 4–7) for each person, chalkboard, chalk, and eraser.

### *Preparation:*

Write the following question on the chalkboard: What blessings come from reading the Book of Mormon?

### *Application:*

Tell your group that in 1986 President Ezra Taft Benson gave an address in general conference titled "The Book of Mormon—Keystone of Our Religion." In that address he promised many blessings to those who read the Book of Mormon. Read the address together as a group. Have class members look for the blessings that President Benson promised. List them on the chalkboard as you read the address. Review the list after you have finished. Encourage your group to study the Book of Mormon so that they can receive the Lord's blessings.

## Object Lesson: "Drawing Nearer to God Through the Book of Mormon"

### *Materials Needed:*

A Book of Mormon, a magnet, and several paper clips.

### *Application:*

Read the sixth paragraph of the Introduction of the Book of Mormon with your class. "Concerning this record the Prophet Joseph Smith said: 'I told the brethren that the Book of Mormon was the most correct of any book on earth, and the keystone of our religion, and a man would get nearer to God by abiding by its precepts, than by any other book.'" Briefly discuss what Joseph Smith meant by this.

Put the magnet in the center of a table. Place the paper clips a few inches away from the magnet. Point out that as we learn the eternal precepts in the Book of Mormon we will gradually grow closer to Heavenly Father and Jesus Christ. Use a toothpick to slowly push the paper clips toward the magnet. As we live by these precepts we will be drawn even closer to them. With the toothpick slide the paper clips into the magnet's field of power. Watch as each paper clip is pulled and fastened to the magnet.

Explain that there is power in the word of God to draw us near him, just as this magnet has power to draw the paper clips to it. Encourage your group to grow closer to Heavenly Father and Jesus Christ through studying and obeying the precepts in the Book of Mormon.

## Additional Enrichment:

### *Hymns:*

- "Book of Mormon Stories," *Children's Songbook,* p. 118.
- "The Iron Rod," *Hymns,* no. 274.
- "As I Search the Holy Scriptures," *Hymns,* no. 277.

### *Scripture Stories:*

- Returning to Jerusalem to get the brass plates (see 1 Nephi 3–5).
- Moroni hides the plates in the Hill Cumorah (see Moroni 1:1, 10:2–5).
- Joseph Smith receives the gold plates (see JS—History 1:47–59).

# Choices

*Choose one or more of the following ideas to enrich your lesson.*

## Object Lesson: "Choices Have Consequences"

### Materials Needed:

A set of dominoes, masking tape, and a marker.

### Preparation:

Place a piece of masking tape across the front of a domino. Use a marker to label it "CHOICE." Put masking tape across the front of ten more dominoes and label each one "CONSEQUENCE."

### Application:

Show your group the domino labeled "CHOICE." Explain that it represents one choice in our lives. Although the choice may seem small it can have many consequences. Discuss the choice to tell a lie. Challenge the group to name as many consequences as they can for telling a lie (feeling guilty, others find out, losing the Spirit, others don't trust you, and so on). Stand up a "CONSEQUENCE" domino for each idea they give. Make sure you place the dominoes closely together in a row. Place the "CHOICE" domino at the beginning of the row and point out that even one small choice can have many consequences. Push the "CHOICE" domino over, toppling the line of dominoes.

Briefly discuss consequences of good choices. What would the consequences be for choosing to tell the truth?

## Activity: "Choosing to Follow Jesus Christ"

### Materials Needed:

Scriptures, chalkboard, chalk, and eraser.

### Preparation:

Draw two vertical lines to divide the chalkboard into three columns. Label the center column "Daily Decisions."

### Application:

As a group, brainstorm decisions that we are faced with each day, such as: whether or not to gossip, finding time to study the scriptures, sharing our testimonies with another, and so on. List their ideas under the center column labeled "Daily Decisions." Read Alma 30:8 as a group. Point out that we may choose between two people to serve: Jesus Christ or Satan. Label the right column "Jesus Christ" and the left column "Satan."

Review each decision individually. Discuss what Satan would want us to do versus what Christ would want us to do. Record these thoughts in the appropriate columns.

Reread Alma 30:8. Help the group to understand that the choice of who we will serve is determined through the decisions we make each day. Draw a large "X" through the column labeled "Satan." Challenge the group to choose the right.

## Object Lesson: "Making Wise Choices"

### Materials Needed:

A box of chocolate-covered candy with an assortment guide.

### Application:

Display the box of candy. Ask the class if they have ever selected a chocolate and then didn't like it when they discovered what was inside. Display the assortment guide and ask how it can be helpful.

Compare this to making good choices. Discuss what resources are available to guide us in making wise choices.

Pass around the box of candy with the assortment guide and allow everyone to choose which chocolate they would like.

## Additional Enrichment:

### Hymns:

- "I'm Trying to Be like Jesus," *Children's Songbook,* pp. 78–79.
- "Come, Follow Me," *Hymns,* no. 116.
- "Do What Is Right," *Hymns,* no. 237.
- "Choose the Right," *Hymns,* no. 239.

### Scripture Stories:

- The Anti-Nephi-Lehies choose to follow the Savior (see Alma 23–24).
- The good Samaritan chooses to help (see Luke 10:25–37).
- The young man who chooses riches (see Matt 19:13–26).

# Example

*Choose one or more of the following ideas to enrich your lesson.*

## Activity: "Jesus Christ Is the Perfect Example"

### *Preparation:*

Write the following on the chalkboard:
"Behold ___ am the _____ ; ___ have _____ an _____ for _____."
Print the following words, in random order, at the top of the chalkboard:
1. I
2. light
3. I
4. set
5. example
6. you

### *Application:*

Allow your class to find the correct place for each word. When class members have finished adjusting the words, have them look up 3 Nephi 18:16 (last part). Discuss what this scripture means. Help your class understand what kind of example Jesus Christ set for us, and what each person must do to follow that example.

## Activity: "I See Examples and Show Examples"

### *Application:*

Explain that examples are all around. Every day each class member can see good examples and bad examples. Help your class understand that Heavenly Father wants us to remember the good examples.

Have your class think of someone who has shown a good example. Without mentioning any names, share what some of those good examples are.

Now have the class think of ways that they can be good examples for other people. Briefly discuss these ideas. Challenge the class members to be good examples to other people.

## Analogy: "The Lighthouse"

Like a beacon in the night, lighthouses have been guiding ships for hundreds of years. As the light reaches out through a stormy night, a lighthouse provides warning of the rocks and shoals that could so easily rip a ship apart. Even on calm nights, when the ocean is as smooth as a mirror, a flashing light will alert a ship's crew of the approaching coastline and prevent a possible tragedy.

Tending the light continues to be a necessary job, and modern conveniences have not lessened the importance of the lightkeeper. Keeping the mirrors or lenses clean and polished is as important now as it was in earlier days. Electricity and incandescent bulbs have replaced less efficient light production but because so many lives depend on him, a lightkeeper must still check and double check equipment on a regular basis.

Like a lighthouse, our examples can become beacons in an ever-darkening world. Even at the times when things seem smooth and calm, many see our examples and veer away from dangerous actions or choices. It is doubly important, therefore, that we constantly check our lives to be sure that we are reflecting the gospel of Jesus Christ in all our doings. Like the lightkeeper, we may never know who is depending on the strength and clarity of our examples to avoid tragedy.

## Story: "President Kimball Learns about Example"

One Sabbath day Spencer W. Kimball, as a member of the stake presidency, visited the Eden Ward in Arizona. As the meeting proceeded he noticed seven boys on the front row of the chapel. It seemed strange to him that each of the seven little boys crossed his right leg over his left knee and then, a moment or two later, all brushed their hair with their right hands. Soon after that, all seven boys leaned lightly on their wrists, supported their faces by their hands, and eventually went back to crossing of their legs again.

President Kimball wondered about it as he tried to think of what he was going to say in the meeting. And then all at once it came to him. Those boys were imitating him!

President Kimball learned an important lesson that day: we must be careful; we may not know when others are watching us and following our example. (See Spencer W. Kimball, "The Davids and the Goliaths," *Ensign,* November 1974, p. 79.)

## Additional Enrichment:

### *Hymns:*

- "I Am like a Star" *Children's Songbook,* p. 163.
- "Shine On," *Children's Songbook,* p. 144.
- "We Are Sowing," *Hymns,* no. 216.

### *Scripture Stories:*

- Elisha follows Elijah (see 1 Kings 19:19–21; 2 Kings 2:1–13).
- Daniel sets an example of prayer for King Darius (see Daniel 6).
- Jacob was an example to Enos (see Enos 1:1).
- The stripling warriors were an example of faith to the Nephite army (see Alma 57:19–27).

# Faith

*Choose one or more of the following ideas to enrich your lesson.*

## Activity: "Ask in Faith"

### Preparation:

Print the following on word strips:
* Remember that
* without faith
* you can do
* nothing;
* therefore
* ask
* in faith.

Place the phrase strips, in random order, on a wall or other display area.

### Application:

Have the class unscramble the phrases until they think it is what the scripture says. Have them look up Doctrine and Covenants 8:10 and talk about the meaning of the scripture.

## Activity: "Who Am I?"

### Materials Needed:

Seven pictures: Adam and Eve (62461), Building the Ark (62053), Joseph is Sold by His Brothers (62525), Mary and Martha (62527), Lehi Prophesying to the People in Jerusalem (62517), King Benjamin (62298), Joseph Smith (62449).

### Preparation:

Write the following names on word strips: Adam and Eve, Noah, Joseph, Mary and Martha, Lehi, King Benjamin, Joseph Smith.

Place pictures on one side of a display area and names on the other. Both should be in random order.

### Application:

Tell your class that there are many stories in the scriptures about people who showed faith in Heavenly Father. Explain that you will read a clue about one of the people in the scriptures and they must guess who that person is. When they guess the name, have them choose the correct picture. Place the name by the picture. Repeat until all the pictures have been identified.

Use the following clues in random order or use any others you choose:

*Adam and Eve:* Even though this couple was banished from their first home, they still had faith that Jesus Christ would pay for their sins through the Atonement.

*Noah:* This man showed great faith by building a large boat, even though it was probably far from any oceans.

*Joseph:* Even when he was sold and put in prison, he still knew that Heavenly Father loved him and would care for him.

*Mary and Martha:* Their faith made them send for Jesus when their brother became ill.

*Lehi:* When the Lord told him that his city would be destroyed, he left his home and traveled in the wilderness with his family.

*King Benjamin:* He taught his people about faith and the plan of salvation in ancient America.

*Joseph Smith:* He knew that Heavenly Father would answer his prayer if he prayed in faith.

# Activity: "The Widow Shows Faith in Elijah"

### *Materials Needed:*

Scriptures for each student and a map of ancient Israel (optional).

### *Preparation:*

Read 1 Kings 17:8–16 and be prepared to answer all questions in this activity.
Print the following questions on a chalkboard:

1. Where did this event take place?
2. When did it happen?
3. Who was there?
4. What happened?
5. How does it apply to me?

### *Application:*

Have your class find 1 Kings 17:8–16 in the Bible. Explain to your class that as you read this scripture reference you will answer the questions that are written on the board. Answer each question. You may desire to use the map to show where Zarephath is thought to have been located (on the Mediterranean coast between Tyre and Sidon). Help your class understand how the Widow's example can teach us about faith.

# Analogy: "The Anchor"

After a sailing ship entered port, one of the first things that happened was the dropping of the anchor. Being securely anchored was essential as the ship's crew went about the tasks of loading, unloading, repairing, and getting ready for the next trip. Mariners knew that, even in a safe harbor, tides might cause a boat to drift out to sea and, once again, be at the mercy of the elements. They also knew that salt water, over time, could cause serious deterioration to even the best anchor, and so extra care was always taken to keep the anchor and its rope or chain in good condition.

Modern technology has replaced the sails and allowed ships to become larger and stronger but the need for a good anchor has never decreased, and a ship's crew still depends on a heavy anchor to keep it secure in its harbor.

Like the anchor, faith helps us remain in a secure harbor, safe from the tides of worldliness that would pull us out into the storms of the natural man. Just as the good condition of an anchor is necessary to a ship's crew, the condition of our faith must be important to us and we must constantly be striving to keep it strong and useable.

## Object Lesson: "Faith Is Believing in Things Not Seen"

### *Materials Needed:*

A room with a door and an assistant.

### *Application:*

Have the assistant step out of the room and close the door. The assistant should tell the class where he is. Ask the class if they can see the assistant or prove where he is. Help your class understand that just because they cannot see someone on the other side of the door does not make them less real.

Liken these things to Heavenly Father. Heavenly Father tells us where he is through scripture and prophets. We can talk to him, and he can talk to us through prayer and the promptings of the Holy Ghost. We cannot see him but we can know he is there through the power of faith.

If time permits, discuss other things that cannot be seen but that we know are there. Use ideas such as oxygen, electricity, wind, and so forth.

## Additional Enrichment:

### *Hymns:*

- "Faith," *Children's Songbook,* pp. 96–97.
- "I Pray in Faith," *Children's Songbook,* p. 14.
- "When Faith Endures," *Hymns,* no. 128.

### *Scripture Stories:*

- King Hezekiah trusts the Lord to save Jerusalem (see 2 Kings 19:10–35).
- Centurion pleads for his servant's health (see Matthew 8:5–13).
- Lehi's family leaves Jerusalem (see 1 Nephi 2:1–6).

# Family

*Choose one or more of the following ideas to enrich your lesson.*

## Activity: "Each Family Member Is Important"

### Materials Needed:

Recipe for cookies and the necessary ingredients.

### Preparation:

Prepare cookies as recipe directs. Make a second batch, omitting an important ingredient, such as salt.

### Application:

Show the group the two batches of cookies that you have prepared. Display the recipe card and the ingredients. Explain how important each ingredient is. If one ingredient is left out the entire recipe can fail. Point out the difference in the cookies.

Liken this to the importance of each member of a family. Everyone contributes to the happiness and success of the family. Discuss how different talents, strengths, and personalities can make family life more enjoyable.

Let each person sample a cookie from each batch to illustrate your objective.

## Object Lesson: "Forever Families"

### Materials Needed:

Two envelopes, two sets of pictures cut out from magazines to represent father, mother, and children. If pictures are not available, simply write the names on separate papers.

### Preparation:

Place a set of family pictures in each envelope. Leave one envelope open, seal the other.

### Application:

Hold up both envelopes and explain that the open one represents a family who has not been sealed for eternity in the temple. The closed envelope represents a family that has been sealed. Death can separate families. Turn the unsealed envelope upside down and gently tap. The family pictures will scatter to the floor. Turn the sealed envelope upside down and shake. Point out that this is similar to the way the sealing power can hold our families together, even after death.

Note: Be sensitive to special circumstances of class members to avoid hurting feelings.

Explain that Heavenly Father values families. He has provided a way for families to be together forever through the sealing power of the temple. Families can be eternal if they live righteously and remain worthy to receive the blessings of being sealed.

# Object Lesson: "Love Strengthens the Family"

### Materials Needed:

Glue, tape, and staples.

### Application:

Display the items and ask what they have in common. (They all hold or bind things together.) Compare this to love in the family. Love is the most important element to strengthen family relationships and hold them together.

# Story: "Margaret McNeil Helps Her Family Cross the Plains"

Margaret and her family joined the Church in Scotland and immigrated to Utah when she was ten years old. While they were crossing the plains, her mother's health was very poor, so Margaret tried to help her as much as she could. Every morning she would get up early and get breakfast ready for the family and milk the cow so that she could hurry and drive her on ahead of the company. She would let her eat in all the grassy places until the company had gone ahead and then would hurry and catch up with them. The cow furnished them with milk, and it was important to see that she was fed as well as possible. Had it not been for the milk the cow provided, the family might have starved.

Margaret was alone most of the time, so she had to get across the rivers as best she could. The cow had a long tail. When it was necessary to cross a river, she would wind the end of the cow's tail around her hand and swim across with her. At the end of each day's journey, she would milk the cow and help prepare the supper.

When the family's food ran out, they had nothing but milk and wild rose berries to eat. They finally arrived in Ogden with thankfulness to Heavenly Father for his protecting care. Margaret McNeil walked every step of the way across the plains and drove the cow, and during a large part of the way carried her little brother James on her back. (See *Remarkable Stories from the Lives of Latter-day Saint Women Volume II,* comp. Leon R. Hartshorn [Salt Lake City, Deseret Book Co., 1975], pp. 9–10.)

# Additional Enrichment:

### Hymns:

- "Love Is Spoken Here," *Children's Songbook,* pp. 190–91.
- "Love at Home," *Hymns,* no. 294.
- "Home Can Be a Heaven on Earth," *Hymns,* no. 298.
- "Families Can Be Together Forever," *Hymns,* no. 300.

# Goals

---

*Choose one or more of the following ideas to enrich your lesson.*

## Activity: "Distractions Interfere with Goals"

### Materials Needed:

A short story of your choice.

### Application:

Ask for a volunteer to read the short story to the class. As the individual reads the story interrupt them several times. (For example, ask them to speak louder, ask if everyone in the back can hear, ask the group if they have heard the story before, have them repeat a sentence, and finally, tell them you don't have time for them to finish it now.)

Have the individual share their feelings about the experience.

Point out that this is very similar to striving to accomplish a goal. Distractions can interfere with our ability and time to complete our objective. Distractions cause us to lose focus of what we are trying to achieve.

Brainstorm with the group, discussing the various distractions that rob us of time or change our focus of what is right.

## Activity: "Goals Give Direction"

### Materials Needed:

An empty box.

### Application:

Have everyone take off their shoes and put them in the box. Mix the shoes up and put them in a pile on the floor. Allow everyone to quickly find their own shoes then return to their seats. Point out how fast they were to complete this task. Ask why it was so easy to find their shoes. (They knew what they were looking for.)

Liken this to goals. As we set specific goals we are more likely to succeed in these areas because we can more easily identify what we are striving for.

## Activity: "Steps to Achieving Goals"

### Materials Needed:

A simple boxed jigsaw puzzle (25 pieces or less), a table or flat working surface, chalkboard, chalk, and eraser.

### *Application:*

Have a member of your group assist in this activity. Give the volunteer the jigsaw puzzle and ask them to put it together. Instruct the group to observe. After the puzzle is completed, discuss the steps that were used in putting the puzzle together. List them on the left side of the chalkboard.

1. Understood what was expected.
2. Organized and sorted pieces.
3. Looked frequently at cover picture.
4. Fit together one piece at a time.
5. Used all the pieces.

Compare this to the steps in setting and achieving goals. On the right side of the chalkboard, write the corresponding phrases that illustrate the same steps for setting goals.

1. Determine goal.
2. List short term steps to complete goal.
3. Have a vision of the outcome.
4. Complete one step at a time.
5. Continue until goal is reached.

## Object Lesson: "Goals—One Step at a Time"

### *Materials Needed:*

Three small rubber balls.

### *Application:*

Select a volunteer from your group. Show them the three balls and explain that the objective is for them to catch all three balls. Stand a few feet apart. Toss all three balls at the same time. Ask the group why the volunteer was not able to catch all of the balls. (Too much to do at one time.)

Toss the balls one at a time and compare the results.

Explain that this is similar to goals. Working on too much at one time is discouraging and unsuccessful. We must carefully select goals and work step by step to achieve them.

## Story: "Heber J. Grant—Determination the Key to Success"

When Heber J. Grant was a boy he wanted to become a bookkeeper for the Wells Fargo and Company bank because it paid more than polishing shoes. He knew that he must improve his writing to have a job like that. At first his penmanship was so bad that two of his friends joked, "That writing looks like hen tracks." "No," said the other friend, "it looks as if lightning has struck an ink bottle." These comments hurt Heber's pride. He decided he would practice until he could write better than his two friends. Later he said that he used carloads of paper practicing writing.

All of this practice helped him to develop the talent. He was eventually called on to write greeting cards, wedding cards, insurance policies, stock certificates, and legal documents. In his day these things were written by hand and not printed. He was even offered a high salary to go to San Francisco as a penman, but he declined. He later taught penmanship and bookkeeping at the University of Deseret. (See David C. Call, "Success—Spiritual and Temporal," in *Grant Oratorical Contest, BYU Speeches* [Provo: Brigham Young University, 30 November 1965], p. 6.)

## Additional Enrichment:

### *Hymns:*

- "Improve the Shining Moments," *Hymns,* no. 226.
- "Today, While the Sun Shines," *Hymns,* no. 229.

# Gratitude

*Choose one or more of the following ideas to enrich your lesson.*

## Activity: "Count Your Blessings"

### Materials Needed:

A bean bag.

### Application:

Gather your class in a circle and toss the bean bag to one of the class members. When they catch it they must name something they're thankful for. Try to give everyone the opportunity to participate.

Help your class understand that these are things that they can thank Heavenly Father for.

## Activity: "Draw Your Gratitude"

### Materials Needed:

Paper and crayons.

### Application:

Give each class member a piece of paper. Have them gather around a table or other flat surface. Tell them to draw a picture of something that they are grateful to Heavenly Father for. After everyone is done drawing, have each class member show their picture and explain why they are grateful to Heavenly Father.

## Activity: "I'm Thankful For . . ."

### Materials Needed:

Building blocks.

### Application:

Gather your class around a table or other solid, flat surface. Have the first class member say "I'm thankful for . . . ," and add a blessing. When the blessing has been stated, place a block on the table. Give each person the opportunity to express a blessing and "build" the house. Repeat this process until (1) there are no blocks left or (2) the blocks fall down.

# Parable: "The Ungrateful Servant"

One day a servant came to his master and said, "O master, you have already given me much but I would be so grateful if you could find a larger room for me to live in."

The master acknowledged his servant's hard work and granted his servant's request. The grateful servant worked harder than ever to show his gratitude. Weeks passed before the servant returned to the master and asked, "Is it possible, my Lord, to receive a few better clothes? It would indeed be a good thing because then others would see how generous you are and would honor you for it."

The wise master looked at the servant thoughtfully and replied, "I will give you some new clothes but not because I desire another's praise. Allow this gift as a reward for your continued obedience and service."

The servant, inwardly rejoicing, bowed from the presence of his lord to await his master's gift. The new clothing, when it arrived, was more than the servant had dared hope for, and he admired them for a long time.

"My master must truly appreciate my worth," he murmured, and from that very day the servant began to honor himself.

Every month the servant would bow before his master and request new gifts and every month the patient master would acknowledge the servant's work and grant his requests.

One day the servant once again petitioned his master; this time for richer food. The master simply looked at the servant and said, "I greatly appreciate all you continue to do for me but all who live within my household, from the greatest to the least, eat the same food. We have no need of such foods," and with that the servant was dismissed.

As weeks passed, the servant continued to think about his request, dwelling on what he had been denied. Twice more he sought his master and twice more the master kindly but firmly denied his request.

Still unable to accept the answer, the servant went to the master again and said, "I do not understand why you must deny me the very thing that so many in the city have. You are hard on me. I can barely keep my life together with what you give me. I work hard for you, barely have time for myself and yet you still will not grant this small request."

"Do you not remember all that I have given you?" exclaimed the master. "Have you so quickly forgotten the many requests I have answered or the gifts I have given? Ungrateful servant, you have deceived yourself."

Sometimes we become so involved with what we need or want that we forget the many blessings and opportunities that Heavenly Father has given us. Even when Heavenly Father gives us an answer that is disappointing, we should always remember what we have been given and acknowledge his wisdom.

# Additional Enrichment:

## *Hymns:*

- "Children All Over the World," *Children's Songbook,* pp. 16–17.
- "Count Your Blessings," *Hymns,* no. 241.
- "My Heavenly Father Loves Me," *Children's Songbook,* pp. 228–29.

## *Scripture Stories:*

- Noah gives thanks to the Lord (see JST Genesis 9:4–6).
- One leper returns in gratitude (see Luke 17:12–19).

# Holy Ghost

*Choose one or more of the following ideas to enrich your lesson.*

## Activity: "Follow the Quiet Voice"

### *Preparation:*

Hide a small item in your classroom.

### *Application:*

After your class has begun, tell them that there is a small item hidden in the room. If you desire, explain what this item looks like. Explain that you will tell them if they are looking in the right place, but they must listen very carefully because you will be talking very softly.

Invite one class member to come forward. Have him find the hidden item by listening to your instructions. Remind him that he can listen only to your words, he cannot look at you. Give directions as quietly as possible.

If time permits, give every class member the opportunity to find the hidden item. To do this, have a member leave the room while it is hidden in a new place. Repeat the above process each time.

When everyone has had the opportunity to participate, talk about how important it was to concentrate in order to hear the quiet voice. Help your class understand how this relates to the Holy Ghost.

## Activity: "Gifts of the Spirit"

### *Preparation:*

Print the following scripture references on individual slips of paper:
- Doctrine and Covenants 11:7 (word 7)
- Alma 18:35 (word 13)
- Doctrine and Covenants 42:48 (words 12, 15, 16, and 17)
- 1 Corinthians 12:9 (word 13)
- Moroni 10:12 (word 10)
- Joel 2:28 (word 25)
- 1 Kings 3:9 (word 15)
- Acts 2:4 (word 16)
- Moroni 10:16 (words 6, 7, and 8)

### *Application:*

Distribute the slips of paper to class members and have them find the scripture reference and indicated word. Ask each class member to read his scripture and then give the reference word. List each word on the board.

When all of the words have been listed, ask if anyone can recognize these gifts. Explain that these are some of the spiritual gifts that we can receive through the Holy Ghost. Help your class understand that although they are gifts of the Spirit, we receive them from Heavenly Father and we can obtain these blessings only if we are obedient and faithful.

Read Doctrine and Covenants 46:26. Remind the class that we should use these special gifts to help other people and always remember who gave them to us. As a class, read Doctrine and Covenants 46:32.

## Object Lesson: "Listen to the Still, Small Voice"

### Materials Needed:

A blindfold.

### Application:

Blindfold one of the class members. Have another class member stand by the door (or a table). Turn the blindfolded person around several times. Ask him to point to the door (or a table). Then have the blindfolded person put his hands at his side. Now, have the other class member softly say, "The door (or table) is here." Have the blindfolded person point in the direction of the voice.

Liken this to the Holy Ghost. In this life sometimes we feel as though we have been blindfolded and spun around until we are no longer sure which way is which. That is when we must listen even more carefully to the still, small voice of the Spirit. The Holy Ghost will always tell us which is the best and safest direction we can go.

## Story: "Elder Seibold Is Guided By the Spirit"

Immediately before the beginning of World War II, the First Presidency became increasingly concerned about the situation in Europe. As hope for a peaceful settlement faded, all missionaries serving in Germany and Czechoslovakia were to be evacuated. President M. Douglas Wood, of the West German Mission, received his telegram Friday morning and had, by late afternoon, notified his missionaries to leave for Holland immediately. On Saturday morning a missionary called to tell President Wood that the Dutch border had just been closed and missionaries would be unable to leave from there. Knowing that the military would soon take over all the railways, President Wood gave Elder Norman G. Seibold the assignment to assist in finding some of the thirty-one missing missionaries and taking them to safety in Denmark.

Leaving the mission home in Frankfurt, Elder Seibold arrived in Cologne after a four-hour trip on the train. Because of the order to evacuate, he had no idea where the missionaries would be found and so President Wood had instructed Elder Seibold to follow the impressions of the Spirit. Although he had not planned on getting off in Cologne, the impression to leave was strong. As he walked among the thousands of people in the station he began to whistle, "Do What Is Right," and immediately located eight missionaries.

In one small community there was a short wait and he felt that he needed to get off the train. As he stepped down he noticed a restaurant on the street and walked inside. There, seated at a table, were two more of the missing missionaries. As the train followed its course, Elder Seibold continued to follow the promptings of the Spirit in every community they passed through. Eventually, he would find seventeen missionaries and receive word that the other fourteen had made it to safety through Holland. (See Richard O. Cowan, *The Church in the Twentieth Century* [Salt Lake City: Bookcraft, 1985], pp. 178–80.)

## Additional Enrichment:

### Hymns:

- "Let the Holy Spirit Guide," *Hymns*, no. 143.
- "Listen, Listen," *Children's Songbook*, p. 107.
- "The Still Small Voice," *Children's Songbook*, pp. 106–07.

### Scripture Stories:

- The Spirit is poured out on the day of Pentecost (see Acts 2).
- The Spirit of the Lord is poured out upon King Benjamin's people (see Mosiah 4:1–3).

# Humility

*Choose one or more of the following ideas to enrich your lesson.*

## Activity: "Scriptures Teach of Humility"

### Materials Needed:

Scriptures for each person in your group, chalkboard, chalk, and eraser.

### Preparation:

Write the following scriptures on the chalkboard, leaving blanks in the appropriate places:
- Matthew 18:4
  Whosoever therefore shall _____ _____ as this little child, the same is _____ in the _____ of _____.
- Ether 12:27
  And if men come unto me I will show unto them their _____. I give unto men _____ that they may be _____; and my grace is sufficient for all men that humble _____ before me; for if they _____ themselves before me, and have _____ in me, then will I make weak things _____ _____ unto them.
- D&C 112:10
  Be thou _____; and the Lord thy God shall _____ thee by the hand, and give thee _____ to thy _____.

### Application:

Instruct the class to use their scriptures to look up the verses on the chalkboard. As a group fill in the blanks. Ask the group to list the blessings that are promised to those that are humble. (To be among those in the Kingdom of Heaven, to have weaknesses become strengths, to receive answers to prayers.) Discuss each verse and its promise.

## Object Lesson: "Humbly Accepting the Lord's Will"

### Materials Needed:

Sugar cubes, a glass of very cold water, and a glass of very warm water.

### Application:

Show the two glasses of water and tell the class that one is filled with very warm water and the other is filled with very cold water. Drop a sugar cube in each glass and briefly stir. Have the class make observations about which dissolves faster.

Compare this to humility. When we are cold or hard hearted we become unwilling to accept Heavenly Father's will in our lives. But if we are warm and teachable we will embrace his direction in our lives.

## Object Lesson: "Humility Helps Us to Become Christlike"

### Materials Needed:

A lump of soft clay and a lump of hardened clay.

### Application:

Demonstrate how the soft clay can be molded into any shape that you desire. Then try to mold the hardened clay. Express the difficulty you are having in shaping the hardened clay. State that the hardened clay is unworkable.

Explain that we are like the clay. When we are humble we can be shaped and molded the way the Lord needs us. If we become stubborn we harden ourselves to the guiding influences of the Lord and we become unworkable. Discuss ways in which we can become more humble.

## Additional Enrichment:

### Hymns:

- "When Faith Endures," *Hymns,* no. 128.
- "Be Thou Humble," *Hymns,* no. 130.
- "More Holiness Give Me," *Hymns,* no. 131.

### Scripture Stories:

- Job remains humble through affliction (see Job).
- Jesus is humble to Heavenly Father's will (see Matthew 26:38–39; Mark 14:34–36; Luke 22:41–42).
- King Benjamin's people believe his words and humble themselves before God (see Mosiah 2–5).

# Individual Worth

*Choose one or more of the following ideas to enrich your lesson.*

## Activity: "Each of Us Is Different"

### Materials Needed:

Paper and crayons.

### Application:

Take your class outside and have each class member select a leaf from the same tree. Return to the classroom and show the class how to make a "rubbing."

Make a rubbing by placing the leaf under the paper. While holding the leaf and paper securely in one place, use a crayon to lightly color over the top of the leaf. This will produce a pattern of the leaf, its veins and other individual qualities, on the paper.

Allow your class to use their own leaves to make rubbings and then compare. Show your class that every leaf is different, even though they came from the same tree.

Liken the leaves to Heavenly Father's children. Even though our spirits came from the same heavenly parents, we are all different. If time permits point out some positive differences in each class member.

## Activity: "Snowflakes and People—Everyone Is Different"

### Materials Needed:

Squares of lightweight paper and scissors for every class member.

### Preparation:

Cut several snowflakes.

### Application:

Display the snowflakes to the class. Point out the differences. Explain to the class that real snowflakes are also different from each other. Heavenly Father gives each of them a beauty all their own.

Tell the class that each person is also different from everyone else. Talk about differences in people. Explain that even though we are all different, Heavenly Father gives each of us special talents and qualities that makes us individuals.

## Activity: "The Premortal Existence Teaches Us Who We Are"

### Materials Needed:

Pearl of Great Price for each person, chalkboard, chalk, and eraser.

## *Preparation:*

Write the phrase "Premortal Existence" in the center of the chalkboard and draw a circle around it. This will be the center of your information wheel. (See illustration.)

## *Application:*

Read Abraham 3:22–28 carefully as a group. Challenge your group to find as many details as possible about our premortal existence from these verses. For each item they name, write it on a spoke of your information wheel. (See illustration.)

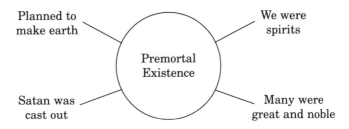

# Activity: "The Worth of Souls Is Great"

## *Preparation:*

Print the following scriptural references on slips of paper:
1. Hebrews 8:12 (word 17)
2. Doctrine and Covenants 15:6 (word 17)
3. Psalm 77:13 (word 12)
4. 1 John 3:2 (word 8)
5. Alma 27:17 (word 21)
6. Isaiah 55:3 (word 11)
7. 3 Nephi 9:22 (word 3)

Print the following scripture on the chalkboard. The solution for this puzzle is found in Doctrine and Covenants 18:10, 13.

"___(1)___ the ___(2)___ of souls is ___(3)___ in the sight of ___(4)___; . . . And how great is his ___(5)___ in the ___(6)___ that ___(7)___!"

## *Application:*

Divide the previously prepared slips of paper among the class. One at a time, have them look up their scripture, read it to the class, and find the puzzle word. If you desire, you can do this in a random order. Fill in the words until the entire phrase has been finished.

Have the class members find Doctrine and Covenants 18:10, 13 in their scriptures. Read the scripture with your class and discuss what it means. Help them understand how important each of them is to Heavenly Father.

## Object Lesson: "We Can Become Like Heavenly Father"

### Materials Needed:

A package of seeds with the picture on front.

### Application:

Show the group the seeds. Explain that these seeds have the potential to become what is pictured on the seed packet. Ask the class, What would you have to do in order for this to happen? Read the planting directions on the package and discuss the various things you would need to do to grow the plant.

Help the group to understand that we are like the seeds. Each of us has the ability to become like Heavenly Father because we are his children. Discuss what things we need to do to nourish the "seeds" within us.

## Object Lesson: "We Have a Heavenly Father"

### Materials Needed:

A picture of a baby and a picture of an adult.

### Application:

Show the group the picture of the baby and its parent. Explain that someday this baby will grow up and be like its parent. Point out that we also have another parent who we want to become like (Heavenly Father). Heavenly Father is the father of our spirits, and we lived with him before we came to our earthly parents. Point out that just as we can become like our earthly parents, we can become like our Heavenly Father also.

## Object Lesson: "We Have Divine Potential"

### Materials Needed:

One apple and a knife.

### Application:

Cut the apple in half, widthwise, and show the inner part. Tell your class that every apple has a similar five-sided star inside that holds seeds. No matter what the condition of the apple is (withered, bruised, or ready for picking), the star and the seeds are still inside.

Explain to your class that we are like the apple. Each of us has the potential (seed) of becoming like Heavenly Father. No matter what adversity or trial we go through, we still have the ability to return to Heavenly Father. Help your class understand that Heavenly Father gave us this opportunity because he loves us.

# Additional Enrichment:

## *Hymns:*

- "Dear To the Heart of the Shepherd," *Hymns,* no. 221.
- "God Is Watching Over All," *Children's Songbook,* p. 229.
- "I'm Thankful to Be Me," *Children's Songbook,* p. 11.

## *Scripture Stories:*

- The Savior eats with Zacchaeus the publican (see Luke 19:2–10).
- One lamb is important to the Shepherd (see John 10:1–18).
- Moses learns of the Lord's purpose (see Moses 1:37–42).

# Jesus Christ

*Choose one or more of the following ideas to enrich your lesson.*

## Activity: "Jesus Showed Us a Pattern for Living"

### Materials Needed:

Pencils.

### Preparation:

Enlarge one of the following patterns and make enough copies for each class member.

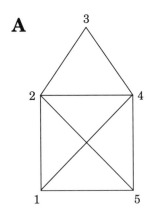

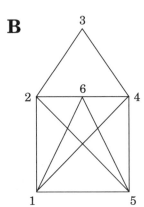

### Application:

Give each class member a copy of the pattern and a pencil. Ask them to trace the design without lifting their pencil or drawing the same line more than once. Give the class one or two minutes to accomplish the task. If one of your class members is able to accomplish it, allow them to help you at the board.

Draw the pattern on the chalkboard, one line at a time, using the following directions. Depending on the age of your class, have them correctly trace theirs as you show them how.

For Pattern A: 1 to 2, 2 to 3, 3 to 4, 4 to 5, 5 to 1, 1 to 4, 4 to 2, and 2 to 5.

For Pattern B: 1 to 2, 2 to 3, 3 to 4, 4 to 5, 5 to 6, 6 to 4, 4 to 1, 1 to 6, 6 to 2, 2 to 5, and 5 to 1.

Help your class understand that it was easier because someone showed them a pattern for how it was done.

Explain that Heavenly Father sent Jesus Christ to show us how to pattern our lives. Tell them that when we follow the Savior's example we will be able to have the Holy Ghost guide and direct us in the right way to live.

## Activity: "Jesus Showed Us How to Be Righteous"

### Materials Needed:

A large bag of various colored beads, string.

### *Application:*

Give each person a length of string. Have the beads in containers within easy reach of everyone. Explain that you are going to show them what to do. They are to watch and carefully follow your example and do exactly as you do.

Select a bead and hold it up for them to see the color. Thread it onto the string and slide it about three-fourths down the length of string. Continue selecting the beads of various colors and threading them on the string. After you have about ten beads, join the two ends of string and tie a knot. Hold up the finished product to allow them to compare theirs.

The finished products should look alike.

What did they do to make a string of beads exactly like yours? (Watch carefully and follow each step closely.) Liken this to following the Savior's example. We must learn of him and his ways. We need to follow his example step by step. If we do this we will become like him.

Briefly discuss the ways we can learn more about Jesus Christ and his example.

## Activity: "We Can Choose to Be Like Christ"

### *Materials Needed:*

A hard, flat surface to draw on, paper, crayons, and a box of flat objects that can be used for crayon rubbings, such as coins, leaves, feathers, cut out geometric shapes, paper clips, greeting cards with raised letters, and so on.

### *Application:*

Pass out paper and crayons. Let everyone select one object from the box to make a crayon rubbing with. Demonstrate how to make a crayon rubbing. Place a flat object under a piece of paper. Unwrap a crayon and lay it flat on the paper. Rub the crayon across the paper several times. This will leave an impression of the item under the paper.

Have group members make their own pictures. Let each person show theirs to the group when it is finished.

Point out that everyone's picture is different. The picture will depend on what they chose to make a likeness of. Liken this to the importance of following the Savior's example in our lives. If we desire to be Christlike we must make sure it is Jesus Christ's example that we are following. Discuss other worldly influences that tempt us to follow their examples.

## Activity: "The Savior Is Our Example in All Things"

### *Materials Needed:*

Display area, six pictures: Jesus the Christ (62572, GAPK 240), John Baptizing Jesus (62133, GAPK 208), Jesus Praying with the Nephites (62542), Boy Jesus in the Temple (62500, GAPK 205), Christ and the Children (62467, GAPK 216), Jesus Healing the Nephites (62541, GAPK 317).

### *Preparation:*

Prepare slips of paper with one of the following words on each: *baptism, prayer, scriptures, service,* and *love.*

Post *Jesus the Christ* picture in the center of your display area.

*Application:*

Read John 13:15: "For I have given you an example, that ye should do as I have done unto you." Discuss the importance of Christ's example for us.

Let a person in your group select a slip of paper and read the word to the group. Have them choose the appropriate picture and invite comments that help us to understand the ways that example helps us. Continue until all five slips of paper have been discussed and pictures posted.

Read John 12:26: "If any man serve me, let him follow me." Encourage your group to serve Jesus Christ by following his example.

## Object Lesson: "The Savior Is the Light We Follow"

### *Materials Needed:*

A sunflower (or picture of one), sunflower seeds, and small plastic bags.

### *Preparation:*

Place a small amount of sunflower seeds in individual plastic bags and seal the bags closed.

### *Application:*

Display the sunflower. Explain to the group how the sunflower got its name: As soon as the sun appears in the morning, the sunflower turns its face toward the sun and follows its path. This simple flower follows the sun's progress all through the day and into the evening, until the sun disappears over the horizon.

Compare this to our loyalty in following the Son of God. Use the following questions to generate a discussion:

How can our focus on following the Savior become distracted?

How can we strengthen ourselves so we do not become weary of following him?

Read John 8:12: ". . . I am the light of the world: he that followeth me shall not walk in darkness, but shall have the light of life." Pass the bags of sunflower seeds out to the group members as a reminder to follow the Son of God.

## Parable: "Jana's Older Brother"

Jana loved Jason, her older brother. When she was very little he always found time to play games with her or take her places. She could count on him to hold her hand or give her a little hug. Jason was someone that Jana always felt safe with.

Today, Jason was taking Jana for a walk in the country. Jana snapped her jacket and doubled checked her shoes and then put her hand in Jason's for today's adventure.

As they walked along the well-worn path, Jason often stopped to look at the leafy trees or shallow brook. Once, they stopped to watch a tiny ant drag a huge crumb back to its nest. It was a marvel to see so many wonderful things.

Once Jana raced ahead, eager to see everything, and Jason called her back and gently reminded her that safety could only be found close to him. If the path became rough Jason would take Jana's hand and help her over the rocks, roots, or hidden dangers on the path, and when she became tired, he carried her on his strong shoulders until she was rested.

As the day wore on, Jason sensed Jana's weariness and knelt down beside her and said, "Jana, do you see that hill?"

"Yes," she sighed, moving closer to her brother.

"Home is just on the other side," he said.

Her eyes brightened at the thought, and she said, "Home! Jason, will it take long?"

"No," he softly replied. "We'll be there soon." And he slowly stood up.

Then Jana reached out for his hand, and together they continued over the last hill to home.

Just like Jason, the Savior is our constant guide through the adventure of life. Loving us, as only a brother might, he answers our questions, guides us, reprimands us as necessary, comforts us, and even carries us when we are weary. Never tiring, he continues to be our companion until, the adventure over, he can deliver us back to our heavenly parents.

We, like Jana, have the choice of walking hand in hand with our elder brother. We can ask questions, receive comfort and guidance, and choose to stay within the safety of his love until we too can return, our hand in his, to our eternal home.

## Additional Enrichment:

### *Hymns:*

- "I'm Trying to Be like Jesus," *Children's Songbook,* pp. 78–79.
- "Come, Follow Me," *Hymns,* no. 116.

### *Scripture Stories:*

- Jesus calling the fishermen (see Matthew 4:18–22).
- Moroni calls upon the people to remember God (see Alma 46).
- Lehi follows the Lord by leaving Jerusalem (see 1 Nephi 1–7).

# Missionary Work

*Choose one or more of the following ideas to enrich your lesson.*

## Activity: "Reflecting the Light of the Gospel"

### *Materials Needed:*

A flashlight with a strong beam, a hand mirror, and small happy-face stickers.

### *Application:*

Briefly discuss our responsibility to share the gospel with others. Liken the gospel of Jesus Christ to the flashlight beam. We are like the mirror, and can reflect his light to others. At times it can be difficult to reach certain individuals, but with time and effort the gospel light can be reflected (or shared) even in the farthest corner.

Quickly demonstrate how the mirror can reflect the flashlight beam to different areas. Keep the flashlight steady, and angle the mirror to transfer the beam. Darken the room. Hold the flashlight and mirror and reflect the beam to someone in the group. Invite that person to come up and use the mirror to reflect the flashlight beam and touch someone else. (Continue to hold the flashlight for them.) When the beam touches someone, it is then their turn to reflect the light to another. Place a happy-face sticker on each person as they are touched by the light. Continue until each person has had a chance to receive the light and reflect it to someone else.

Discuss the importance of sharing the gospel with everyone. How would you feel if you had been left out?

## Object Lesson: "Sharing the Gospel"

### *Materials Needed:*

Treats for your group.

### *Application:*

Begin by taking a treat for yourself. Eat it and describe how good it tastes. Ask someone to describe how good it tastes. (They won't know.) Ask why that person doesn't know. (They have not tasted it.)

Explain that the gospel is like this treat. Others can see that you have it, but until you offer to share it they cannot enjoy it for themselves. Share the treat with the entire group.

## Story: "Brigham Young, a Faithful Missionary"

Many of the Saints in the city of Nauvoo had become sick from malaria caused by the mosquitoes along the Mississippi River. At this time, Brigham Young and his fellow Apostles were called to preach the gospel in England. The men, as well as their families, were very sick. Brigham Young said, "My health was so poor that I was unable to go thirty rods to the river without assistance. . . . I left my wife sick, with a babe only ten days old, and all my children sick and unable to wait upon each other." (*Manuscript History of Brigham Young,* ed. Elden Jay Watson [Salt Lake City: Smith Secretarial Service, 1968], p. 50.) But he left his family in the care of the Lord with the assurance that they would be taken care of.

He was in England for one year. As president of the mission he and his companions baptized between 7,000 and 8,000 people, distributed 5,000 Books of Mormon, 3,000 hymn books, and 50,000 tracts. A shipping agency was also established, and nearly a thousand converts were emigrated to Nauvoo. (See *Encyclopedia of Mormonism,* s.v. "Brigham Young.")

## Additional Enrichment:

### *Hymns:*

- "We'll Bring the World His Truth," *Children's Songbook,* pp. 172–73.
- "Because I Have Been Given Much," *Hymns,* no. 219.
- "Called to Serve," *Hymns,* no. 249.

### *Scripture Stories:*

- Ammon: example of a great missionary (see Alma 17:18–39; Alma 18–19).
- Calling the fishermen (see Matthew 4:18–22; Mark 1:16–20).
- Feed my sheep (see John 21:15).

# Obedience

---

*Choose one or more of the following ideas to enrich your lesson.*

## Activity: "I Can Choose to Be Obedient"

### Application:

Hold up your hands and show your class how you can move your fingers. Explain that you can choose how your hands will move. Help your class understand that although you can choose to move your own hands and fingers you cannot make that choice for anyone else.

Have your class members hold their hands up. Ask them to do something with their hands (open and close fingers, spread fingers wide, touch the thumb and pointer fingers, and so forth). Do several things with your class. Praise them for being obedient.

Tell the class that, just as they chose to be obedient with their hands, they can also choose to be obedient with their bodies and minds.

## Activity: "Prophets Are Examples of Obedience"

### Materials Needed:

Five pictures: Daniel Refusing the King's Meat and Wine (62094), Daniel in the Lion's Den (62096), Lehi's Family Leaving Jerusalem (62238), Samuel the Lamanite on the Wall (62370), Moroni Hides the Plates in the Hill Cumorah (62462).

### Preparation:

Put all of the pictures on display.

### Application:

Point to one of the pictures on the display area. Ask the class to identify the prophet and what he did to show his obedience to Heavenly Father. Repeat until all of the pictures have been talked about.

Tell the class that prophets show us, by their examples, how to choose the right. Help them understand that the prophets know that obedience keeps us safe from Satan.

## Object Lesson: "Obedience Is a Protection for Us"

### Materials Needed:

A pair of overshoes, a hat, a pair of gloves, and a coat.

### Application:

Show the overshoes to the class. Have them explain how the shoes are used and what kind of protection they offer. Discuss each item of clothing the same way. Help the class understand that each of the pieces of clothing was made specifically to protect some part of the body. Ask what would happen if only part of the clothing was worn.

Liken the clothing to the commandments that Heavenly Father gives us. Explain that, like the clothing, commandments are given for our protection. Some commandments protect us in one way and others protect us in another. Help your class understand the protection that comes when all of God's commandments are kept.

## Story: "The Mormon Battalion Is Obedient"

Shortly after the Saints were expelled from Nauvoo, the United States government sent Captain James Allen to Brigham Young, requesting 500 men for the war with Mexico. Although the body of the Saints had little desire to assist a government that allowed murder and theft, President Brigham Young recognized the opportunity as a blessing from the Lord and called upon the men to commit themselves to this endeavor.

Before leaving, the battalion officers met with the Quorum of the Twelve Apostles. They were charged to remember the Lord, revere his name, pray, strictly keep the commandments, and see that no life be taken unless absolutely necessary. If they would do these things, they were promised that their lives would be spared.

As they traveled from Council Bluffs to Southwestern California they often dealt with sickness and a lack of food and water. Heat and sandy trails slowed their progress but they never fought in a major battle, and each was preserved to be reunited with their loved ones. (See *Encyclopedia of Mormonism,* s.v. "Mormon Battalion.")

## Additional Enrichment:

### Hymns:

- "Keep the Commandments," *Children's Songbook,* pp. 146–47.
- "I'll Go Where You Want Me to Go," *Hymns,* no. 270.
- "I Want to Live the Gospel," *Children's Songbook,* p. 148.

### Scripture Stories:

- Saul makes excuses for his disobedience (see 1 Samuel 13:8–14).
- Jonah learns obedience (see Jonah 1, 2, and 4).
- Esther obeys Mordecai (see Esther 4–7).
- The Lord commands Nephi to build a ship (see 1 Nephi 17).

# Prayer

*Choose one or more of the following ideas to enrich your lesson.*

## Activity: "Learning About Prayer Through the Scriptures"

### Materials Needed:

The following pictures: the First Vision (62470; GAPK 103), Enos Praying (62604; GAPK 305), Jesus Praying in Gethsemane (62175; GAPK 227), Jesus Praying with the Nephites (62542).

### Preparation:

Read and be prepared to discuss the following scripture stories: the First Vision (Joseph Smith—History 1:11–20), Enos praying (Enos 1), Jesus praying in Gethsemane (Luke 22:39–46), Jesus praying with the Nephites (3 Nephi 17).

### Application:

Display all four pictures. Tell each story. Discuss what these stories have in common (prayer). Ask questions about each story to illustrate the different things that were prayed for. Joseph Smith was praying for instruction and guidance. Enos was praying for forgiveness and for the welfare of his people. In Gethsemane Jesus was praying for strength to do Heavenly Father's will. Amongst the Nephites, Christ prayed for the people.

Compare this to our prayers. Challenge your group to utilize all the important aspects of prayer.

## Activity: "The Lord's Prayer"

### Materials Needed:

A copy of the Lord's Prayer (Matthew 6:9–13) for each person to read and mark, and marking pencils.

### Preparation:

Read and be prepared to discuss the Lord's prayer.

### Application:

Pass out copies of the Lord's prayer and marking pencils. Read the prayer as a group. Explain that Christ was teaching the people how to pray by using this prayer as an example. Point out that we can also learn how to enrich our own prayers from it. Have group members take turns locating and underlining the important things we should pray about. Be sure to include the following: to praise and express gratitude to Heavenly Father, to ask for his will to be done, to ask for our daily needs, to be forgiven, to forgive others, and to resist temptation. Using this as a guide, challenge the group to identify an area in which their prayers may be lacking and strive to improve it.

## Object Lesson: "Prayer Gives Us Power to Keep the Commandments"

### *Materials Needed:*

An electric blow-dryer, an electric clock, an electric cassette player with a tape, and access to an electrical outlet.

### *Application:*

Discuss what each item is used for and demonstrate how they work. Point out that each is carefully designed to fulfill a certain purpose. However, the ability to do that is dependent on one important thing: power. Without electrical power the items would be of little worth.

Compare this to our lives and the power that prayer can give us to serve Heavenly Father and keep his commandments.

## Object Lesson: "Prayer—A Guiding Light"

### *Materials Needed:*

A powerful flashlight, lamp, or other source of light.

### *Application:*

Demonstrate how to use the light source you brought. Point out its ability to assist us to better see in the dark so that we can identify dangers and better accomplish our tasks.

Use this to illustrate the similarity to prayer. Prayer gives us the "light" to see temptations and other dangers. Prayer is a light that gives us guidance and instruction.

## Additional Enrichment:

### *Hymns:*

- "A Child's Prayer," *Children's Songbook,* pp. 12–13.
- "Did You Think to Pray?" *Hymns,* no. 140.
- "Sweet Hour of Prayer," *Hymns,* no. 142.

### *Scripture References:*

- Joseph Smith's First Vision (see JS—History 1:1–20).
- Jesus teaches the Nephites to pray (see 3 Nephi 18:15–24).
- The publican humbly prays (see Luke 18:10–14).

# Prophets

*Choose one or more of the following ideas to enrich your lesson.*

## Activity: "Latter-day Prophets"

### Materials Needed:

Pictures of eight latter-day prophets.

### Preparation:

Write the following letters on eight pieces of plain white paper: P, R, O, P, H, E, T, and S.

Place the lettered squares on a display area, with a picture over the top of each letter. If you are working with an older class display the letters and pictures in a random order.

### Application:

Have a class member identify one of the prophets. If time permits, have a brief discussion about events in that prophet's life. Take the picture down and uncover the letter square. Repeat until all of the letter squares have been uncovered. If you have chosen to mix the letters have your class arrange the letters in the proper order.

## Activity: "Latter-day Prophets Were Children Too"

### Materials Needed:

A picture of each prophet.

### Preparation:

Place the pictures in random order at the bottom of a display area.

### Application:

Show the pictures and tell your class that these are the men that Heavenly Father chose as his prophets in the latter days. Use the following clues to help them understand that, even though they grew up to be special servants of Heavenly Father, these men were once children who played games, read books, performed chores, and were just like most other children.

Give a clue about a prophet and have the children guess which prophet it applies to. When the children guess the correct prophet, place the picture in the correct order at the top of the display area. Following are sample clues:

1. *Joseph Smith.* Even though he walked with a slight limp, he loved to participate in all kinds of sports. Neighboring farmers were eager to hire him because he was a hard worker, even after a day in the hot sun. (See Susan Arrington Madsen, *The Lord Needed a Prophet* [Salt Lake City: Deseret Book, 1996], pp. 4–7.)

2. *Brigham Young.* Because his mother was very ill, he helped his family by making bread, churning butter, and helping to make the meals. Every day, before he went out for his daily chores, he would carry his mother to a chair in front of the fireplace. (Ibid., p. 27.)

3. *John Taylor.* Once another boy tore up his kite and he became so angry that he said a word he shouldn't have. When he realized what he had said he cried all the way home because he thought Heavenly Father would never forgive him. (Ibid., p. 46.)

4. *Wilford Woodruff.* He was one of the first people in his area to learn to make fishing flies with feathers and hooks. The fish liked them so well that he once caught two fish on one hook. (Ibid., p. 61.)

5. *Lorenzo Snow.* His grandfather's military stories excited him so much that he talked his sister into sewing a military uniform for him. He called it his freedom suit and spent many hours imagining himself as the leader of a victorious army. (Ibid., p. 73.)

6. *Joseph F. Smith.* Even though he was seven years old, he needed to be the "man" of the family, so he drove his family's ox team to Winter Quarters. On their rest day, however, he would pick gooseberries or throw lumps of dirt at garfish in the streams. (Ibid., pp. 92–94.)

7. *Heber J. Grant.* When he was younger, the other boys laughed because he couldn't hit or throw the ball very far. He practiced every day after school and work and eventually he became good enough to play on the team that won the territorial championship. (Ibid., p. 109.)

8. *George Albert Smith.* When he was a small child he came down with typhoid fever. The doctor told his mother to give him only coffee to drink but he believed in the Word of Wisdom and asked for a priesthood blessing instead. The next day he was able to play with his friends. (Ibid., p. 125.)

9. *David O. McKay.* One year his summer job was as a newspaper carrier for the *Standard.* His job was to carry the paper to a nearby mining town. Because he rode his horse all the way, a round trip took him from seven in the morning until five o'clock in the evening. (Ibid., pp. 140–41.)

10. *Joseph Fielding Smith.* Beginning when he was ten years old, he would hitch the horse to the buggy and drive his mother to help whenever babies were born. He would do this in the middle of the night and in all kinds of weather, but because of it he learned to offer service wherever or whenever it was needed. (Ibid., pp. 158–59.)

11. *Harold B. Lee.* When he was a deacon, he helped take care of the church house by washing the chimney, sweeping the floor, filling the lamps, and chopping wood for the stove. (Ibid., p. 172.)

12. *Spencer W. Kimball.* He was known for being smart, happy, and short but he could outwrestle almost any boy that was near his size. He used to say, "I sit tall but stand short." (Ibid., p. 189.)

13. *Ezra Taft Benson.* After a week of farm chores his family would often go to Bear Lake for a day of fishing, swimming, and picnicking during the summer. During the winter he would tie a rope on the saddle horn and ski behind his horse. (Ibid., p. 208.)

14. *Howard W. Hunter.* Although he lived in the city, he loved to visit a nearby wooded area and watch the birds build their nests. He had a special place in his heart for abandoned or mistreated animals, especially cats, and took many home to be cared for. (Ibid., pp. 222–23.)

15. *Gordon B. Hinckley.* His family lived in town during the school year and spent their summers at a home in the country. During those summer times he helped plant gardens and irrigate and plant trees. The family would often sleep outside and try to find the North Star in the sky. (Ibid., pp. 242–43.)

## Activity: "Prophet Time Line"

### Materials Needed:

Twelve pictures: Jesus Christ (62572), Building the Ark (62053), Abraham Taking Isaac to Be Sacrificed (62054), The Crossing of the Red Sea (62100), Daniel in the Lion's Den (62096), John Preaching in the Wilderness (62132), Lehi and His People Arrive in the Promised Land (62045), Moroni Hides the Plates in the Hill Cumorah (62462), The Prophet Joseph Smith (62002), Brigham Young, Ezra Taft Benson, Gordon B. Hinckley.

### Preparation:

Place the picture of the Savior in the center of the display area. Place the other eleven pictures, upside down and in random order, at the bottom of the display area.

### Application:

Tell the class that Heavenly Father has always given us prophets to guide and direct us. Remind them that some prophets lived before Jesus was born and others were called as prophets after his birth.

Ask a class member to come forward and choose one of the pictures from the bottom of the display. Identify the prophet and have the class tell you if he was a prophet during the time before or after Christ's birth. Place the pictures of Noah, Abraham, Moses, Daniel, and Lehi to the left of the picture (indicating before Christ was born) and pictures representing John the Baptist, Moroni, Joseph Smith, Brigham Young, Ezra Taft Benson, and Gordon B. Hinckley to the right (indicating after Christ was born). If time permits tell a story about one or two of the prophets.

## Additional Enrichment:

### Hymns:

- "Come, Listen to a Prophet's Voice," *Hymns,* no. 21.
- "Follow the Prophet," *Children's Songbook,* pp. 110–11.
- "Latter-day Prophets," *Children's Songbook,* p. 134.

### Scripture Stories:

- Naaman obeys a prophet's instruction (see 2 Kings 5).
- Daniel interprets a dream for Nebuchadnezzar (see Daniel 2:16–45).

# Repentance

*Choose one or more of the following ideas to enrich your lesson.*

## Activity: "Learning from the Example of Enos"

### *Preparation:*

Read and be prepared to discuss Enos.
Use the following questions to make two-sided wordstrips:

**Side A**
1. How did Enos's attitude about repentance help him?
2. How did Enos's faith assist him?
3. How did Enos feel about his brethren, the Nephites, after he repented? About the Lamanites?

**Side B**
1. How can our attitude affect our repentance?
2. How can faith help us in the repentance process?
3. How do we feel about our loved ones after repentance? About our enemies?

### *Application:*

Post the three wordstrips (with side A facing forward). Read the questions. As a group, read Enos. (Instruct the members of your class to ponder the questions as you are reading.) Discuss their thoughts on each question.

Turn the wordstrips over to side B. Discuss each question and its personal application to repentance.

## Activity: "Repentance Brings Joy"

### *Materials Needed:*

Newspapers, and pre-moistened handwipes.

### *Application:*

Give everyone in your group a large sheet of newspaper. Challenge them to make a very small, tight ball out of the newspaper. Point out that wrinkling and working the newspaper first will help to soften it and make it more pliable. Collect all of the newspaper balls. Display one and help the group to understand how making the newspaper balls is similar to earth life. During our lives we are often exposed to worldliness and wickedness. We may find that we have given in to temptation and sinned. We will feel unclean. Instruct your group to look carefully at their hands. They will notice the residue of newsprint.

Heavenly Father does not want us to feel unclean. Through the power of the Atonement we can repent and feel clean and pure again. Pass out the premoistened hand wipes. After cleaning their hands, ask them how it feels. The relief of repentance brings us joy.

Challenge the group to utilize the power of repentance in their lives.

## Object Lesson: "Becoming Clean Through Repentance"

### *Materials Needed:*

Two clear glass pitchers, water, pebbles, and a strainer.

### *Preparation:*

Fill one pitcher with water, add several pebbles.

### *Application:*

Display the pitcher of water with the pebbles. Liken this to our lives and the sins we commit. Heavenly Father has provided a way for us to cleanse our lives of these sins. It is called repentance. Place the strainer over the empty glass pitcher. Pour the water through the strainer. Observe how it filtered the pebbles out of the water. Repentance works similarly to remove sins from our lives. We can become clean again through repentance.

## Object Lesson: "Repentance Relieves the Burden of Sin"

### *Materials Needed:*

Several heavy books.

### *Application:*

Invite a member of your group to help with this demonstration. Have the person stretch their arms out in front of them, with their elbows locked and palms up. Place a book on the palms of their hands. Explain that when we sin it is like a burden that we carry with us. Each sin we commit adds to that burden. Place another book on top of the first one. Give several examples of sin: lying, gossiping, anger, and so on. With each example add another book to the stack. Ask the volunteer to explain how they are feeling. Would the burden eventually make them miserable? Ask your group what would help the person to feel better (putting the books down). How can we put down the burden of sin? (repent). Have the person put down the books. Ask them to describe how it feels to set the load down (relieved). Liken this to the feeling repentance brings.

## Parable: "Emily's Rocks"

### *Materials Needed:*

A backpack and four to six large rocks.

### *Application:*

*As you tell this story, place the rocks into the backpack in the suitable places.*

Emily was going on a hike with her family. She had spent many days wondering what wonderful things she would see. She even decided to take her backpack like a real hiker. Things would be wonderful because her father and her older brother, Richard, left earlier to set things up at the campsite.

There were so many beautiful things to touch and see at the beginning of the hike that Emily soon fell behind the group. She always kept them in sight, however, and it never took long to catch up. When they stopped to look at the busy ants she saw a beautiful red rock and, as everyone else went on, she stopped to pick it up and put it in her backpack.

The trail seemed to get even more interesting as she found, not just one, but three more rocks of unusual shape and color. Then, further on she found two more. Each time she added those wonderful rocks to her backpack the rest of the family hiked a little further ahead. She kept track of the group, however, and ran to make up the distance whenever she fell behind.

The longer she went on, the heavier the backpack became until, at last, the backpack grew so heavy that she could only watch as everyone else disappeared around the bend. Too tired to go on, she sat down, opened her backpack, and peered inside. It was the stones that weighed her down, but they were so beautiful and interesting that she knew she couldn't leave them.

*Show the heavy backpack to your class and have one or two members come up and try it on. Ask if they would like to carry it for a long time. Briefly discuss what Emily could do to solve her problem.*

Emily felt alone and, as the quiet minutes passed, she wondered if anyone missed her. Even the forest began to look dark and gloomy, and she began to wonder how she would ever find her family again. Just as she was starting to cry, she looked up and saw her older brother, Richard, walking down the path and smiling at her.

"Dad sent me back to find you," he said. "Are you all right?"

No one had ever looked better, and Emily ran to give her brother a big hug. Tearfully, she explained what happened as they sat down under a big tree. Richard sat down, opened her backpack, took out each rock, and examined them carefully.

He explained that the rocks, as interesting as they seemed, needed to be left behind before she could go on. He talked about the beautiful camping spot that had been chosen and the wonderful things they would do there. Then he reminded her how much she was loved and how worried their parents would be until her safe return.

Emily decided she didn't need the rocks after all. In fact, as she looked, they really weren't as interesting as she remembered.

## Additional Enrichment:

### Hymns:

- "Repentance," *Children's Songbook,* p. 98.
- "Savior, Redeemer of My Soul," *Hymns,* no. 112.
- "Come unto Jesus," *Hymns,* no. 117.

### Scripture Stories:

- Saul's change of heart (see Acts 9:1–22).
- The prodigal son returns (see Luke 15:11–32).
- King Benjamin's people become sons and daughters of Christ (see Mosiah 5).

# Reverence

*Choose one or more of the following ideas to enrich your lesson.*

## Activity: "The Nativity—A Feeling of Reverence"

### Materials Needed:

Pictures: The Birth of Jesus (62116; GAPK 200), The Nativity (62495; GAPK 201), The Announcement of Christ's Birth to the Shepherds (62117; GAPK 202).

### Preparation:

Be prepared to read the account of the birth of Jesus (Luke 2:1–20).

Make arrangements for a pianist to play "Silent Night" softly in the background as you read. (You may want to practice together.) Or, if a piano is not available, play a tape of the music.

### Application:

Display the pictures of the events surrounding the birth of Jesus. Quietly read the prepared scriptures as the pianist plays "Silent Night."

Ask your group to imagine that they were there on the night of his birth. What would their feelings be? (Love, awe, humility, and so forth.) Explain that those are all feelings of reverence. Those are the same feelings that we should have in our meetings, during the sacrament, at the temple, while reading the scriptures, during prayer, and so on.

Help the group to understand that as we ponder the Savior's life it will increase our feelings of reverence.

## Object Lesson: "A Reverent Atmosphere"

### Materials Needed:

A pot, a large serving spoon, a delicate goblet or glass, and a small teaspoon.

### Application:

Take the large spoon and bang the pot loudly several times. Then use the teaspoon to carefully tap the glass, producing a delicate ringing sound.

Compare this to irreverent/reverent behaviors and attitudes. Irreverent actions can distract and interfere with the feelings of the Spirit. Reverent actions create an atmosphere that invites the Spirit.

## Object Lesson: "Reverence Is Important"

### Materials Needed:

A small piece of thread.

## *Preparation:*

Place a piece of thread on the front of your shirt or jacket prior to your lesson. It should be a color that will easily stand out on your clothing (for example, white thread on a black jacket).

## *Application:*

Begin by having a brief discussion on reverence. Use the following questions to assist:
- In what ways can we show reverence?
- How does a reverent/irreverent atmosphere affect us?

At an appropriate point, stop and ask if anyone noticed the thread. Find out if it bothered them. You will find that a good portion of the class will have been so distracted by the thread that they paid little attention to your lesson.

Help them to understand that if something as little as a thread can distract us, how much more distracting is talking, tapping our foot, or any other form of inappropriate behavior or appearance? Our lack of reverence can distract ourselves and others from feeling the Spirit.

# Story: "Jesus Christ Appears to Lorenzo Snow in the Temple"

One evening Lorenzo Snow was visiting with one of his granddaughters in the Salt Lake Temple. When she was ready to leave, he followed her into the corridor. Suddenly he said, "Wait a moment, Allie, I want to tell you something. It was right here that the Lord Jesus Christ appeared to me at the time of the death of President Woodruff." He took another step, held out his left hand, and continued, "He stood right here, about three feet above the floor. It looked as though He stood on a plate of solid gold." President Snow then described the Savior's appearance and his beautiful white robes. (LeRoi C. Snow, "An Experience of My Father's," *Improvement Era,* September 1933, p. 677.)

Use this story to illustrate the sacredness of the temple and how it should affect our feelings of reverence.

# Additional Enrichment:

## *Hymns:*

- "Reverence Is Love," *Children's Songbook,* p. 31.
- "To Think about Jesus," *Children's Songbook,* p. 71.
- "Oh, May My Soul Commune with Thee," *Hymns,* no. 123.
- "God Is in His Holy Temple," *Hymns,* no. 132.

## *Scripture Stories:*

- Jesus cleansing the temple (see Matthew 21:12–16; John 2:13–17).
- Moses and the burning bush (see Exodus 3).

# Scriptures

*Choose one or more of the following ideas to enrich your lesson.*

## Activity: "Learning about People of the Scriptures"

### Materials Needed:

A world map, string or yarn, and nine pictures: Moses and the Burning Bush (GAPK 107), Joseph Resists Potiphar's Wife (GAPK 110), Daniel in the Lion's Den (GAPK 117), John Preaching in the Wilderness (GAPK 207), Jesus Praying in the Garden of Gethsemane (GAPK 227), Mary and the Resurrected Lord (GAPK 233), King Benjamin Addresses His People (GAPK 307), Samuel the Lamanite on the Wall (GAPK 314), and Jesus Teaching in the Western Hemisphere (GAPK316). These pictures may be replaced with others of your choosing.

### Preparation:

Arrange the world map on the display area. Place the pictures, in random order, on both sides of the map. At the edge of each picture connect a string and allow one end to hang until the game begins.

### Application:

Ask your class to tell you about each picture. Briefly discuss each story and gospel principle. Help your students understand that the Bible and Book of Mormon took place in two basic parts of the world: the western and eastern hemispheres. Show them on the map where these two general areas are.

Have class members identify which continent the story took place in and connect the string to the appropriate area. When all the pictures have been identified, remind your class of the reality of these people of the scriptures.

## Activity: "Reading the Scriptures Helps Us Know What to Do"

### Preparation:

Print the following scriptural references on slips of paper:
1. Jacob 3:2 (word 21)
2. Matthew 24:35 (word 9)
3. Psalm 46:8 (word 2)
4. Doctrine and Covenants 5:6 (word 13)
5. Doctrine and Covenants 8:2 (word 5)
6. 1 Nephi 7:12 (word 18)
7. Isaiah 34:16 (word 2)
8. Abraham 3:25 (word 12)

Print the following scripture on the chalkboard. The solution for this puzzle is found in the last part of 2 Nephi 32:3.

___(1)___ upon the ___(2)___ of Christ; for ___(3)___, the ___(4)___ of Christ will ___(5)___ you all ___(6)___ what ___(7)___ should ___(8)___.

### *Application:*

Divide the previously prepared slips of paper among the class. One at a time, have them look up their scripture, read it to the class, and find the puzzle word. Fill in the words until the entire phrase has been finished.

Have the class members find 2 Nephi 32:3 in their scriptures. Read the scripture with your class and discuss what it means.

## Object Lesson: "The Scriptures Measure Truth"

### *Materials Needed:*

Yardstick and four other items that could be used to measure a line (a piece of paper, string, elastic thread, yarn, and so forth). Measuring items should be smaller than the line and of differing lengths.

### *Preparation:*

Draw an eighteen-inch line on the chalkboard before your lesson begins.

### *Application:*

Have volunteers use the four assorted items to measure the line. Write their answers underneath the line. For instance, 2 and 2/3 sheets of paper, 5 lengths of string, 2 lengths of stretched elastic thread, and so forth. Point out the varying measurements and how they differ. Help your class understand how difficult it would be to use these measurements in recreating the line.

Now use the yardstick and measure the line. Explain how much easier it is to measure the line. Discuss why.

Liken the yardstick to the scriptures. Help your students understand that the scriptures are an unwavering measurement of truth. Discuss how the scriptures can be a tool to help us discern and discover truth.

## Story: "Martha Finds Peace from the Scriptures"

Ever since Martha's family had moved to Stiller, she had felt unhappy and lonely. Before, when they lived in Jonestown, she had many friends and never felt this way. Mother told her that soon she would make new friends and she wouldn't feel so lonely.

One Saturday Martha and her older brother Greg were working in the garden and talking about how Martha felt.

"Greg, I miss all my old friends a lot. I don't think I'll ever find new friends here."

Greg thought about what she said as they finished planting the row. Then, after deciding to take a break, she sat under a nearby tree while he went for water from the house. When he returned he brought a set of scriptures, as well as a cool drink. "My seminary teacher told us that we can find answers for every problem in the scriptures," he said after he sat down. "I'd like to share one of my favorites with you."

He thumbed through the book quickly and read from Doctrine and Covenants, " 'Draw near unto me and I will draw near unto you; seek me diligently and ye shall find me; ask, and ye shall receive; knock, and it shall be opened unto you'" (Doctrine and Covenants 88:63).

"Brother Erickson taught us that we could come closer to Heavenly Father by reading our scriptures and praying every day. I know this works, Martha. I may not have any answers for you but I know Heavenly Father does. If you really give him a chance he'll help you."

"Now," Greg said, "We have a garden to finish!"

That night Martha looked up "Happiness" in her topical guide and found a special scripture in John. "If ye know these things, happy are ye if ye do them" (John 13:17). Later, Martha prayed to Heavenly Father for an answer to her problem. As she thought, she remembered how helping other people always made her happy.

All that week Martha did things that helped other people. At home she tried harder to help without being asked. At school she tried to smile and say hello to everyone, and at church she tried to listen to the lesson and think of the Savior as she partook of the sacrament.

Before she knew it, she felt less lonely and closer to her Heavenly Father. As she helped others, her unhappy feelings were replaced with an inward joy, and she felt happier to be with her new friends in Stiller.

If you would like, use these discussion questions following this story:
- What did Martha's older brother do to help with her problem?
- What did Martha do to find a solution to this problem?
- How did the scriptures help Martha find a solution?

## Additional Enrichment:

### *Hymns:*

- "As I Search the Holy Scriptures," *Hymns,* no. 277.
- "The Iron Rod," *Hymns,* no. 274.
- "Tell Me the Stories of Jesus," *Children's Songbook,* p. 57.
- "Search, Ponder, and Pray," *Children's Songbook,* p. 109.

### *Scripture Stories:*

- Josiah honors the book of the covenant (see 2 Kings 22–23).
- Nephi returns for the brass plates (see 1 Nephi 3–5).
- Joseph Smith seeks an answer in the scriptures (see Joseph Smith History 1).

# Service

*Choose one or more of the following ideas to enrich your lesson.*

## Activity: "Drawing Closer to the Savior Through Service"

### Materials Needed:

Two individual binder rings, a large picture of Christ attached to a poster board, three sheets of tissue paper the size of your poster board, clear cellophane, and an easel.

### Preparation:

Prepare the visual aid by punching two holes in the top of the poster board and in corresponding places on the tissue paper and cellophane. Layer the cellophane directly on top of the picture, followed by the three sheets of tissue paper. Attach the picture, cellophane, and tissue sheets together with the binder rings. Place this on an easel for the lesson.

### Application:

Introduce your activity by reading John 15:12–14. Explain that Christ's life greatly reflected service, and he has admonished us to follow this example. As we offer Christlike service we will draw closer to him.

Smooth the tissue paper against the poster board. Ask what they can see. A faint outline of the Savior will be visible. Ask for a member of your group to share an experience of when he offered service. When he has finished, ask if it helped him to feel closer to Christ. Pull back the first layer of tissue paper. They will notice the picture is a little clearer. Repeat this process for the two remaining sheets of tissue paper, each time noting how much clearer their view of Jesus Christ is.

All that will cover the picture at this point is the cellophane. Use this to illustrate how thin the veil can become and how close we can draw to the Savior through Christlike service.

## Object Lesson: "Service Strengthens Relationships"

### Materials Needed:

A comb and some small bits of tissue.

### Application:

Have a member of your group use the comb on their hair. Then demonstrate how the comb can pick up the bits of tissue. As the comb is used it develops static electricity. This power can be used to draw things towards it.

Compare this to service. As we use our time and abilities to serve others, a feeling of charity develops. This draws us together and strengthens our relationships.

## Activity: "Service Uplifts Others"

### *Preparation:*

Contact class members and ask them to be prepared to share a personal experience of service and how it uplifted them. This can be an experience that they offered service or that service was offered to them.

### *Application:*

Take turns sharing service-related experiences. Be sure the class relates how the experiences made them feel.

Conclude by helping the group see the benefits of service in the lives of all.

## Story: "President George Albert Smith Exemplifies Service"

President Heber J. Grant's daughter relates the following story of an occasion when President George Albert Smith was traveling back from a convention, and she saw him looking across the aisle at a young mother and her children, surrounded by luggage. He felt a need to talk with her to inquire after her welfare.

President Grant's daughter said, "In a few minutes President Smith was over talking to the young mother. He came back to our seat and said, 'Yes it is just as I thought. The little mother is going on a long journey; I have looked at her ticket. I can't understand why the man who sold it to her didn't know a better route for her to travel. As it is she will have a long wait in Ogden and again in Chicago. I have her ticket and am going to get off in Ogden and see if I can't get it changed so she can make other connections and not have the long wait in Ogden and Chicago.'"

President Smith jumped off the train as soon as it stopped and had the young mother's ticket changed to afford her greater convenience. (In Arthur Ray Bassett and Leon R. Hartshorn, "George Albert Smith: On Reaching Out to Others," *New Era,* January 1972, p. 52.)

## Additional Enrichment:

### *Hymns:*

- "A Poor Wayfaring Man of Grief," *Hymns,* no. 29.
- "Because I Have Been Given Much," *Hymns,* no. 219.
- "Have I Done Any Good?" *Hymns,* no. 223.
- "Scatter Sunshine," *Hymns,* no. 230.

### *Scripture Stories:*

- Jesus heals the sick and feeds the multitude (see Matthew 14:13–21).
- The widow feeds Elijah (see 1 Kings 17:8–24).

# Standards

*Choose one or more of the following ideas to enrich your lesson.*

## Activity: "Be an Example in All You Do"

### Preparation:

Print the following on wordstrips:
- Dating
- Dress/Appearance
- Friendship
- Honesty
- Language
- Movies/Books
- Music/Dancing
- Sexual Purity
- Sabbath Day

Place all wordstrips face side down on a display area.

### Application:

Have a class member choose one of the wordstrips and read it to the class. Talk about choices that must be made in each area and discuss ways that each of us can be a righteous example. Repeat for every wordstrip. If questions arise, use *For the Strength of the Youth* as a resource.

## Object Lesson: "Keeping Standards, Even Under Pressure"

### Materials Needed:

Children's modeling clay.

### Application:

Give the clay to a person in your group and instruct them to shape something out of it. When they are finished, have them show it to the group. Encourage them to change their design by giving several suggestions, such as: try making it thinner, bend it a little, flatten it, and so on. (The finished project should differ greatly from their original design.)

Use this to illustrate that outside pressure often causes us to change our standards. We must be strong to resist the temptation of giving in to this pressure.

## Object Lesson: "Moral Purity Is Essential to Spirituality"

### Materials Needed:

A beat-up, dirty, or rusty hanger; a new, unused hanger; and a beautiful, delicate article of clothing.

*Application:*

Display the hangers and the clothing. Ask on which hanger you should hang the clothing. Discuss why.

Explain that when we allow our bodies or minds to be used in unrighteous or worldly desires or attitudes, our spirituality becomes corrupted. Just as we would not want to hang delicate clothing on this hanger (hold up dirty hanger), the Lord does not wish to cloak us with sacred, beautiful experiences, such as priesthood ordinances, until our lives are in order and we are fully ready to receive them.

## Object Lesson: "Standards Are a Protection"

### *Materials Needed:*

Sixteen bricks.

### *Preparation:*

Label the bricks with the following words:

| | |
|---|---|
| Appearance | Movies |
| Books | Music |
| Dancing | Obedience |
| Dating | Prayer |
| Dress | Repentance |
| Friendship | Scriptures |
| Honesty | Sexual Purity |
| Language | Sabbath Day |

### *Application:*

Briefly discuss the walls that biblical people used to protect themselves from enemies. Talk about the importance of the walls being well made with bricks or stones that were solid and without flaw.

List some enemies that we face today (pornography, drugs, lying, and so forth). Bring out the bricks, one at a time, and begin to build a wall. Talk about each topic and how it can strengthen our spirituality. Help your class understand that the gospel acts as the mortar that holds our standards in place and makes the wall even stronger.

## Object Lesson: "Standards Are Contagious"

### *Materials Needed:*

Chalk dust.

### *Application:*

After chalking your hands, show them to the class. Offer to shake hands with each class member. Discuss why shaking hands would or would not be a good idea.

Liken the chalk dust to standards. Explain that we often take the standards of those we associate with. Heavenly Father wants us to have standards that will help us return to him. He knows how important it is for our friends to have the same standards. Help your class understand that a righteous standard begins with each of us, individually. We can choose the kind of standards that we want to have.

## Parable: "The Precious Pearl"

Three pearls, although not overly large, were set into rings and given by a loving father to his three daughters. He gave each a ring and told them to keep the rings safe, for they would always remind them of home during their stays in the far city. Then, with kind and loving words, he sent them on their way and encouraged them to return when their visits were finished.

The oldest daughter, upon arriving in the far city, was entranced with the intricate and expensive jewelry sold in the city. In days she became dissatisfied with her plain pearl ring and traded it for glittering and intricate jewelry that had taken her fancy, and then she went to live in the jeweler's quarter.

The second and third daughter mourned the loss of their sister and vowed to treasure their pearl rings all the more. They comforted each other and thought often of home until the day that a tall man approached the second daughter and, with words of comfort and flattery, spent the day in conversation with her.

Days turned into weeks until, finally, the third daughter began to notice a change in her sister. One evening, as the second daughter was leaving in her brightest finery, the third daughter asked where she was going.

"To be with my tall man," was her reply and she waved her hand.

"My sister," the third daughter cried, "where is the ring from father?"

"I gave it to my tall man so that we can be happy in the city," and her laughter rang through the night air as she left her weeping sister.

Time passed, and the third daughter grew in grace and beauty. Her gentle simplicity endeared her to others and brought her many friends. She often gazed at the little ring, remembering the peace and love of home and resolving never to lose her precious treasure.

It was with great joy when, one happy day, a handsome man came into her life. He valued the lovely third daughter and treated her with great love, always honoring her and her pearl ring as though they were treasures of his own.

They, and their friends, returned that very week to the home of her father. Seeing her beloved parents, she ran to meet them, arms outstretched, pearl ring shining.

Personal purity, or chastity, is like a pearl of great worth. This precious treasure is a power that, when used correctly, brings us close to Heavenly Father and helps us return to our heavenly home with honor.

## Additional Enrichment:

### *Hymns:*

- "As Zion's Youth in Latter Days," *Hymns,* no. 256.
- "Hum Your Favorite Hymn," *Children's Songbook,* p. 152.
- "The Lord Gave Me a Temple," *Children's Songbook,* p. 153.
- "Sweet Is the Peace the Gospel Brings," *Hymns,* no. 14.

## *Scripture Stories:*

- Daniel and his three friends refuse the king's food (see Daniel 1:8–20).
- Moroni stands for freedom and righteousness (see Alma 46:11–24).
- Peter will not take money for his priesthood power (see Acts 8:9–24).

# Standing for the Right

*Choose one or more of the following ideas to enrich your lesson.*

## Activity: "Courage to Stand Alone"

### Materials Needed:

Paper, pen, chalkboard, chalk, and eraser.

### Preparation:

Write the following question on *one* slip of paper:
What is the color of snow?
On four other slips of paper write the following question:
What is the color of the sky?
Fold each paper.

### Application:

Have five volunteers stand in front of the class. Give each person one of the prepared, folded slips of paper. Tell them not to show their papers to anyone else. Instruct them to read the question on their papers. Explain that you will read a list of answers. When the correct answer to their question is read, they are to sit down.

Read the following answers: green, blue, gray. Only one person should be left standing. Ask them why they are still standing up. (Because their answer has not been read.)

Ask the person who is left to share how it feels to be the only one standing. Have them read their question. Why did they stand when everyone else was sitting? (Because they knew they were right.)

Discuss the importance of standing up for what is right. What can we do to develop more courage and strength to stand for the right? List these ideas on the chalkboard.

## Object Lesson: "Be an Example of Standing for the Right"

### Materials Needed:

A magnifying glass and a coin.

### Application:

Pass the magnifying glass and coin around to each class member. Give them the opportunity to look closely at the coin. Point out that the magnifying glass helps us to see important details on the coin.

As members of The Church of Jesus Christ of Latter-day Saints we are under close scrutiny. Others watch us closely. As we strive to stand for the right it will serve as a powerful example to those who are watching.

## Object Lesson: "Showing the Path to Others"

### *Materials Needed:*

A reflector from a bike or other object (single reflectors can be purchased at most hardware stores).

### *Application:*

Show the class the reflector. Reflectors are so named because they "reflect" light from another light source. Reflectors serve two purposes. First, they keep you from danger, such as going off the road or hitting another object. Second, they can mark the proper course to follow.

As members of The Church of Jesus Christ of Latter-day Saints we, in a sense, are reflectors. We reflect the love and truth of the gospel. As we stand for the right we will help keep others from danger. Our examples can help other people stay on the right path.

## Story: "Joseph F. Smith—Young Man of Courage"

Joseph F. Smith was traveling with a company of men. They stopped to camp one afternoon. While Joseph went to gather firewood, a group of drunken men rode into camp, cursing and swearing to kill any Mormon that came in their path. Some of the other men in Joseph's company hid in the brush down by the creek. But Joseph walked back into the camp to deposit his wood. One drunken man with a pistol in his hand said it was his duty to kill every Mormon he met. He demanded of Joseph in a loud, angry voice, "Are you Mormon?" Joseph ignored the gun aimed at him, looked the ruffian in the eye, and answered, "Yes, siree; dyed in the wool; true blue, through and through."

This surprised the man, and he grasped Joseph's hand and said, "Well you're the _____ _____ pleasantest man I ever met! Shake, young fellow, I'm glad to see a fellow that stands up for his convictions." (See Joseph Fielding Smith, *Life of Joseph F. Smith: Sixth President of The Church of Jesus Christ of Latter-day Saints* [Salt Lake City: Deseret News Press, 1938], p. 189.)

## Additional Enrichment:

### *Hymns:*

- "Dare to Do Right," *Children's Songbook,* p. 158.
- "Let Us All Press On," *Hymns,* no. 243.
- "True to the Faith," *Hymns,* no. 254.

### *Scripture Stories:*

- Daniel refuses the king's wine and meat (see Daniel 1).
- Daniel in the lions' den (see Daniel 6).
- Abinadi testifies to King Noah (see Mosiah 11–17).

# Talents and Gifts

*Choose one or more of the following ideas to enrich your lesson.*

## Activity: "Talents Can Build the Kingdom"

### Preparation:

Write a note to each class member about specific talents they have. Be sure to include talents such as compassion, listening, communication, leadership, and so forth.

Write a list of talents on the chalkboard. Make sure that each class member has a talent in that list.

### Application:

Discuss how each of the listed talents can help other people and build the kingdom. Help your class understand that every talent is equally important. At the end of the class give each class member his or her note.

## Object Lesson: "All Talents Are Important"

### Materials Needed:

A picture of a rainbow.

### Application:

Talk about how rainbows can be very different. Some are longer or larger or brighter, but each has a beauty of its own. Have the class identify all the colors in the rainbow, and explain that each color is important. Discuss what it would be like to do without one color.

Explain that talents are like the colors of the rainbow. Talents differ from person to person, but all talents are important. Briefly discuss different types of talent (singing, listening, sharing, leadership, and so forth). Help your class understand how empty the world would be if we did not improve or share our talents.

## Object Lesson: "Discovering Our Talents"

### Materials Needed:

A small object to hide on each class member. Use objects such as a piece of yellow thread, a safety pin, a small pencil, a bobby pin, and so forth.

### Preparation:

List the hidden objects on a piece of paper. Make a copy for every class member.

Before class begins, take each class member aside and "hide" one of the objects in plain sight. For instance, hide a safety pin on a shirt cuff, a bobby pin through a buttonhole, or a pencil behind an ear.

### *Application:*

Hand each member of your class a list. Tell them that each of the objects is hidden in plain sight. As they find the hidden object, they should cross it off their list. When all the objects are found they should sit down. Give a time limit of two minutes.

Liken the objects to talents. Help your class understand that, like the objects on the list, talents must be looked for. Explain that some are easier to find than others and some are not found without the help of others. Talk about how to find talents.

## Object Lesson: "Using Talents to Build the Kingdom"

### *Materials Needed:*

One match.

### *Application:*

Show the match to the class and discuss how fire can be used to help or to harm people. Help the class understand that fire is very helpful but that it is dangerous when it is not used in the right place or in the correct way.

Liken fire to the talents we have been given. Explain that every talent has the potential to help people become closer to Heavenly Father. Help them understand that misuse of talents can also lead us away from our eternal goals. Discuss these ideas.

## Object Lesson: "We Should Expand Our Talents"

### *Materials Needed:*

A bottle of unpopped popcorn and a large bowl of popped popcorn.

### *Application:*

Hold up the bottle of unpopped popcorn. Ask the class if it can be eaten as is. Is there a better way to eat it? What must be done to make it better? Explain that when we apply heat the unpopped popcorn becomes bigger and better.

Liken the popcorn to our talents. Until we apply work and effort, talent remains a tiny kernel inside. It is only after we strive to improve it that it expands and becomes better. Briefly discuss what could happen if we did not develop our talents. Take out the bowl of popcorn and share with your class.

## Additional Enrichment:

### *Hymns:*

- "Every Star Is Different," *Children's Songbook,* pp. 142–43.
- "Improve the Shining Moments," *Hymns,* no. 226.

### *Scripture Stories:*

- Joseph organizes and administers (see Genesis 39:3–6, 21–23; 41:38–43).
- Solomon is given wisdom (see 1 Kings 3:6–14).

# Temples

*Choose one or more of the following ideas to enrich your lesson.*

## Activity: "Temples Around the World"

### Materials Needed:

Pictures of ten different temples from around the world, a large world map, colored pushpins, and a corkboard.

### Preparation:

Display the world map on the corkboard.

### Application:

Show the pictures of the various temples one at a time. Let class members try to guess which temple is on each print. Use a colored pushpin to mark each temple location on the map. Point out that temples are built around the world to offer all worthy members of the Church the opportunity to partake of temple ordinances and blessings.

## Object Lesson: "Benefits of Being Prepared"

### Application:

Have your group imagine that they have been invited to the home of someone they have always admired and looked up to. Explain that they live in a magnificent home, and you have been invited to a special dinner with them. What things would you do to prepare? (Discuss dress, grooming, being prepared for conversation, and so on.) Ask how you would feel to go there unprepared. How would those feelings be different if you had made the effort to prepare?

Liken this to preparing to go to the temple. What things do we need to do to prepare to go to the temple? What things should we do to truly be in tune spiritually? How will this preparation affect your experience at the temple?

## Object Lesson: "Preparing to Go to the Temple"

### Materials Needed:

A packaged brownie mix, a baking pan, foil, and prepared brownies.

### Preparation:

Place the unopened brownie mix in a baking pan and cover it with foil. Bake another batch of brownies, cut up, and place in a container. Place the foil-covered pan in your room where it will be noticeable. Keep the prepared brownies out of sight.

*Application:*

Display the pan and tell the group you have a special treat for them. Unwrap the pan and show them the packaged brownie mix. Express your disappointment that it wasn't ready for them. Liken this to being prepared to attend the temple. Discuss things we should be doing to be ready and worthy to attend the temple.

Conclude by sharing the brownies that were prepared earlier. Being prepared and worthy to go to the temple will bring us happiness and fulfillment. Failing to prepare will bring disappointment to ourselves and others.

# Story: "President Kimball— The Importance of Temple Marriage"

President Spencer W. Kimball told the following true story.

"A few years ago a young couple who lived in northern Utah came to Salt Lake City for their marriage. They did not want to bother with a temple marriage, or perhaps they did not feel worthy. At any rate, they had a civil marriage. After the marriage they got into their automobile and drove north to their home for a wedding reception. On their way home they had an accident, and when the wreckage was cleared, there was a dead man and a dead young woman. They had been married only an hour or two. Their marriage was ended. They thought they loved each other. They wanted to live together forever, but they did not live the commandments that would make that possible. So death came in and closed that career. They may have been good young people; I don't know. But they will be angels in heaven if they are. They will not be gods and goddesses and priests and priestesses because they did not fulfill the commandments and do the things that were required at their hands.

"Sometimes we have people who say, 'Oh someday I will go to the temple. But I am not quite ready yet. And if I die, somebody can do the work for me in the temple.' And that should be made very clear to all of us. The temples are for the living and for the dead only when the work could not have been done. Do you think that the Lord will be mocked and give to this young couple who ignored him, give them the blessings? The Lord said, 'For all contracts that are not made unto this end have an end when men are dead' (D&C 132:7)." (In Conference Report, Japan Area Conference 1975, pp. 61–62.)

# Story: "Heber J. Grant and Lucy Stringham Marry in the Temple"

When Heber J. Grant and Lucy Stringham wanted to get married, the Salt Lake Temple had not yet been completed. The only temple available at that time for endowments and sealings was the St. George Temple. A trip from Salt Lake City to the St. George Temple would be long and hard because it meant days of travel by carriage or wagon through a dry and dusty area.

They wanted to begin their marriage in the temple, but many of their friends encouraged Brother Grant to be married by a stake president or bishop and wait to be sealed until the Salt Lake Temple was complete. They were often reminded of the difficulty of the journey, but they chose to make the trip and be married for time and eternity.

The trip was long and hard because the roads were very bad, but after arriving in St. George they were sealed in the temple.

A few years later, before the Salt Lake Temple was completed, Sister Grant died. Heber J. Grant was grateful that he did not listen to those who tried to convince him to wait. He knew that through the power of the priesthood his beloved wife was sealed to him for eternity. (See Heber J. Grant, *Gospel Standards,* comp. G. Homer Durham [Salt Lake City: *The Improvement Era,* 1941], pp. 359–60.)

## Additional Enrichment:

### Hymns:

- "I Love to See the Temple," *Children's Songbook,* p. 95.
- "High on the Mountain Top," *Hymns,* no. 5.
- "We Love Thy House, O God," *Hymns,* no. 247.

### Scripture Stories:

- Parable of the Ten Virgins (see Matthew 25:1–13).
- Prayer at the dedication of the Kirtland Temple (see D&C 109).
- Vision shown to Joseph and Oliver at the Kirtland Temple (see D&C 110).

# Temptation

*Choose one or more of the following ideas to enrich your lesson.*

## Analogy: "Temptation Is Like a Web"

The spider carefully spun its web until at last the pattern was complete. So cleverly were the strands placed that the trap was almost invisible. Web completed, the spider withdrew to patiently lie in wait.

The day passed; one tiny quarry after another avoided the entrapment until the gentle brown moth blundered in. The little moth struggled in the entangling web until at last it was held tight, at the spider's mercy.

Like a spider, Satan carefully weaves his traps, making some almost imperceptible. He then withdraws to patiently wait for an unsuspecting victim to become trapped in his wicked schemes.

Unlike the moth, we can free ourselves from Satan's snares through the power of repentance. No matter how tightly we may be entangled, the sacrifice of the Savior can help us to become free again.

## Object Lesson: "Avoiding Temptation"

### Materials Needed:

Ground pepper, a bowl of water, and a small amount of liquid dishwashing detergent.

### Application:

Begin this object lesson by talking about the importance of avoiding sin and fleeing from its presence as quickly as possible. Help your class understand that sometimes the best way to avoid temptation is to leave its presence.

Place the bowl where the water can be easily seen by the entire class. Sprinkle the pepper liberally onto the water. Drop a drop of liquid soap into the middle of the water. The pepper will rapidly separate to the outside of the bowl.

Explain to the class that we must be like the pepper and quickly turn away from anything that might cause us to yield to temptation.

## Object Lesson: "Temptations Can Pull Us from the Course"

### Materials Needed:

Compass and a small magnet.

### Application:

Demonstrate to the group how the compass works. Explain that the needle always points to the magnetic north. Using this compass as a guide will keep you from getting lost and help you travel to your desired destination.

However, even the compass can be "pulled" from the right direction. Bring the magnet close to the compass, and let the class observe how the needle is pulled off the right course. Point out that this is similar to the way in which we become distracted from the straight and narrow path. We must stand up for the right and refuse those things that tempt us to go off course. Talk about things that can help us continue to choose the right.

## Object Lesson: "Understanding Deception"

### *Materials Needed:*

Three glasses of water, punch flavoring, sugar, salt, and ice cubes.

### *Preparation:*

Place punch flavoring into all of the water glasses. Add sugar to one glass (enough to make it flavorful), salt to the second, and leave the third glass without salt or sugar. Add water and stir until completely dissolved. Put a few ice cubes into each of the three glasses.

### *Application:*

Have your class look at the glasses of punch. Tell them that each of the glasses is different from the others. Have them guess what the difference could be. Do not commit to any answer. Ask a volunteer to come forward and give him the "sugared" punch. Have him smell it and then drink it. Ask the class if they have figured out what the difference is.

Ask a second volunteer to come forward and have him select a glass and take a drink. Have him describe what he has tasted. Ask a third volunteer to come and sample the third drink and have him describe the taste.

Explain to your class that temptation is like the punch. It may look the same as the sweet punch but, instead, can be bitter to the taste. Help them understand that Satan uses deception to make bad things look good. He wants us to be confused enough to fall into his traps. Talk about ways we can discern good from evil.

## Additional Enrichment:

### *Hymns:*

- "I Believe in Being Honest," *Children's Songbook,* p. 149.
- "School Thy Feelings," *Hymns,* no. 336.
- "True to the Faith," *Hymns,* no. 254.

### *Scripture Stories:*

- Joseph turns away from temptation (see Genesis 39:7–20).
- Helaman convinces the people of Ammon to remember their covenant (see Alma 53:10–14).

# Testimony

*Choose one or more of the following ideas to enrich your lesson.*

## Activity: "A Strong Testimony Reminds Us of God's Love"

### Preparation:

Write the following letters on the chalkboard:
HLUOAVUEUWHAOUFUHWAGUOADUW

### Application:

Remind your students that testimonies can help them remember all that Heavenly Father has given them, and that by doing the things necessary to strengthen our testimony, we become even more aware of Heavenly Father's love for each of us.

Have class members name ways to strengthen our testimony (prayer, reading scriptures, attending meetings, keeping commandments, etc.). When a class member correctly identifies a way to strengthen a testimony, erase every letter "A" in the word. When another way is named, erase every "U." Repeat the process with the letters "W" and "H." At this point, the phrase "LOVE OF GOD" should still be on the chalkboard.

## Object Lesson: "A Testimony Keeps Us Safe"

### Materials Needed:

A small piece of bark from a tree (remove bark from a dead branch).

### Application:

Show the bark to your class. Briefly discuss why a tree has bark (to protect it from disease, insects, weather, and so forth). Talk about what can happen to a tree if it loses too much of its bark.

Liken the bark to our testimony and talk about how it can help protect our spirituality. Talk about how a strong testimony can sustain us in times of turmoil and can keep us from giving in to temptations and doubts. Help your class understand that without a testimony we can become susceptible to the ways of the world.

## Activity: "How to Gain a Testimony"

### Materials Needed:

A small treat for your group, index cards, pen, chalkboard, and chalk.

### Preparation:

Write the following clues on three separate index cards:

1. There is a treat hidden in this room for you to share with the class.
2. You may ask the teacher *yes* or *no* questions to give you clues of its location.
3. You will have to search to find it.

Before your lesson, hide a small treat in the room.

### *Application:*

Ask a member of your group to assist you. Give him the clue cards and have him read the cards aloud to the group. Assist as needed. When the treats are found, share them with the group. Briefly discuss the steps that were used to find the treats. (Gaining a desire to look for it, reading the instructions, asking the teacher questions, and searching.)

Read Moroni 10:3–7 as a class. Explain that Moroni gave us the guidelines to obtaining a testimony. Identify the steps and write them on the chalkboard. Compare this to searching for the treats. What would happen if the instructions had not been read? What happens if scriptures are not read? Neglecting even one step can keep us from gaining a testimony.

## Object Lesson: "A Testimony Keeps Us Steadfast"

### *Materials Needed:*

An electric fan, a piece of paper, a fist-sized rock, and scriptures.

### *Preparation:*

Place the fan on a table and have it plugged into an electrical outlet before your lesson. Arrange the paper about two feet in front of the fan. (Make sure the air flow from the fan will hit the paper.)

### *Application:*

Explain that the fan is like the adversities in our lives. The sheet of paper represents our life. Turn on the fan. What happens? The paper is blown away from the force. Discuss how adversity can cause us to falter or give up.

Point out that a testimony of Jesus Christ and the gospel is like an anchor that will keep us firm and unmovable. Place the large rock on top of the paper. Liken it to a testimony. Turn on the fan. Discuss what happens.

Read Helaman 5:12 together as a group: "And now, my sons, remember, remember that it is upon the rock of our Redeemer, who is Christ, the Son of God, that ye must build your foundation; that when the devil shall send forth his mighty winds, yea, his shafts in the whirlwind, yea, when all his hail and his mighty storm shall beat upon you, it shall have no power over you to drag you down to the gulf of misery and endless wo, because of the rock upon which ye are built, which is a sure foundation, a foundation whereon if men build they cannot fall."

## Object Lesson: "A Testimony Guards Against Sin"

### *Materials Needed:*

A hard boiled egg, egg dye, spoon, and paper towels.

### *Application:*

Display the boiled egg. Liken the shell to our testimony. Point out that we must protect and nourish our testimonies to keep them strong. Our testimony strengthens us in times of temptations. If we neglect our testimonies, Satan has more opportunities to deceive us. Read D&C 10:33 as a group.

Crack the egg shell and peel a small piece away. Put the egg in the container of egg dye. Discuss the various ways to strengthen our testimony while the egg soaks (sharing it, prayer, fasting, obedience and so on).

Remove the egg from the dye and peel it. Dye will have seeped in through the crack and stained part of the egg. A weak testimony also allows temptations to seep into our lives.

## Parable: "The Lawn Mower"

All summer long George used his lawn mower to keep his grass trim and neat. As the weeks passed George began to think about changing the oil and cleaning the spark plugs, but since the mower was running well he figured that there would be plenty of time later. Then, as the autumn rains began, George went to put his lawn mower away.

Realizing that he would have to move a few things first, he quickly moved the lawn mower into a corner and promised himself to take care of it the next day. Unfortunately, the rain soon turned to snow and temperatures dropped before George was able to fulfill his mental promise.

At first, each day would bring a new promise to care for the snow-covered machine, but soon even that faded from his memory. Before George knew it, spring arrived, the lawn became green again, and the lawn mower gradually began to appear through the snow.

It took only a moment for George to discover that his machine no longer worked and that a costly trip to the repair shop would be necessary to repair the damages.

Often we take our testimonies for granted—postponing routine upkeep and maintenance, even placing it in the midst of life's storms without adequate protection. If we neglect to care for our testimonies we could find ourselves, at some critical point, unable to use them. Often the resulting spiritual damage may take extensive repair before enabling us to use and benefit from our testimonies once again.

## Additional Enrichment:

### *Hymns:*

- "I Know My Father Lives," *Children's Songbook,* p. 5.
- "I Know That My Redeemer Lives," *Hymns,* no. 136.
- "Testimony," *Hymns,* no. 137.

### *Scripture Stories:*

- Abinadi remains firm in his testimony even unto death (see Mosiah 16–17).
- Alma the younger repents and gains a testimony (see Mosiah 27 and Alma 36).
- Joseph Smith's testimony helps him deal with persecution (see Joseph Smith— History 1:21–26).

# Thoughts

*Choose one or more of the following ideas to enrich your lesson.*

## Activity: "Cultivating Good Thoughts"

### *Materials Needed:*

A variety of hearty flower seeds, potting containers, and soil for each person in your group.

### *Application:*

Display the various seed packets. Read the descriptions and look at the pictures on each packet. Let each person choose which flower seeds they would like to plant. Assist them in this procedure as needed.

Liken this to choosing to have good thoughts. First, you must carefully select those things you will plant in your mind: scriptures, uplifting movies, good books, wholesome music, and so on. Good thoughts will be grown from these types of "seeds."

Discuss the care that the seeds will need: water and sunlight. Challenge them to take home their planted seeds and nourish them. As they care for the seeds they will be reminded to carefully select, plant, and nourish seeds for good thoughts in their lives.

## Activity: "Negative Thoughts Are Hard to Get Rid Of"

### *Materials Needed:*

A permanent black marking pen.

### *Application:*

Conduct a brief discussion about the importance of guarding against bad influences in our lives. Brainstorm items that can be harmful to our thoughts: inappropriate videos, music, books, magazines, and so on. Point out that all of these things leave thoughts in our minds that can be hard to get rid of.

Use the permanent marker to make a *small* dot on the back of their hands. Liken it to the marks that are left in our mind when we allow ourselves to be exposed to things that are inappropriate. Once these thoughts are planted they can be very difficult to erase. Challenge them to consider this as they try to wash off the black spot later.

## Object Lesson: "Bad Thoughts Linger"

### *Materials Needed:*

A new sponge (light colored), red or blue food coloring, and a large bowl of water.

### *Application:*

Explain to the group that the mind is like a sponge. It quickly absorbs everything that it is exposed to. Soak the sponge in the bowl of water and then squeeze out the extra water to demonstrate how much our minds can absorb. Once those things are in our minds they can be very difficult to eliminate.

Display the food coloring, and explain that it is like the negative influences that we experience. Have the group give some examples, such as: inappropriate jokes or language, videos, music, magazines, and so on. Place a few drops of food coloring on the damp sponge for each negative influence that is mentioned. All of those things lead to bad thoughts. When we try to get those bad thoughts out of our minds it can be very hard. Squeeze the sponge to show how little comes out. Rinse the sponge and squeeze it again to show how the bad thoughts can continue to linger for a long time. Encourage your group to be selective in the things they allow to influence their thoughts.

## Object Lesson: "Thoughts Lead to Actions"

### *Materials Needed:*

A container of water.

### *Application:*

Display the water. Ask the group what would happen if you put the water in the freezer? (It would turn to ice.) What would happen if you heated it up on the stove? (It would boil.) The water is influenced by the atmosphere it is placed in. Use this to illustrate that our thoughts are also influenced by the things we are exposed to. Briefly discuss.

## Additional Enrichment:

### *Hymns:*

- "To Think about Jesus," *Children's Songbook,* p. 71.
- "Jesus, the Very Thought of Thee," *Hymns,* no. 141.

### *Scripture Stories:*

- Amalickiah's thoughts to be king lead to evil, murder, and his death (see Alma 47–51).
- Joseph F. Smith ponders the scriptures and has a vision (see D&C 138).

# BASIC
# TOOLS

# The First Tool of Teaching Is Preparation

*"Therefore, prepare thy heart to receive and obey . . ."*
*—Doctrine and Covenants 132:3*

The success of every lesson is dependent on the time and effort a teacher puts in to personal gospel study and preparation to receive the Spirit (see Doctrine and Covenants 42:14). Consider the following object lesson as you think about the necessity of personal preparation.

## Object Lesson: "Personal Preparation Is Essential to a Successful Lesson"

### Materials Needed:

Several toothpicks, rubber bands, and one pencil.

### Application:

Take a toothpick and bend it. Tell your class that it would be easy to break. Show them that even when two or three toothpicks are held together they can still bend or break.

Now, using the rubber bands, bind the toothpicks to the pencil. Show the class that it is extremely difficult to bend or break the toothpicks.

Liken the toothpicks to teaching techniques. No matter how well you tell a story, do an activity, or read a quote, it is personal preparation the brings the Spirit to a lesson. Briefly discuss what things help us prepare personally (reading scriptures, praying, attending meetings, and so forth).

Although preparation is probably not obvious to many class members, it is nevertheless most important. Good preparation gives any lesson a good foundation and prepares a teacher, through the Spirit's guidance, to become an instrument in teaching the gospel of Jesus Christ.

# Organizing Tools

---

*"Organize yourselves; prepare every needful thing . . ."*
*—Doctrine and Covenants 88:119*

Organization need not be overwhelming. In fact, it can simplify the material and make a lesson easier to give. Organizing can help you recognize your resources and determine what should be used. Consider the following object lesson as you think about the importance of organizing.

## Object Lesson: "Organization Helps Us Prepare to Teach"

### *Materials Needed:*

A brightly patterned piece of material, buttons of varying colors (these should all be about the same size), and several small plastic bags.

### *Application:*

Show the material to the class. Tell them that you are making an article of clothing from this material. Explain that the pattern calls for several colors of buttons. Inform them that the buttons are very important because they will greatly enhance the pattern.

Place all the buttons on a table where they can easily be seen, and sort according to basic colors. If time permits allow your class to assist with the sorting.

When the sorting is complete, go through the colors and match the buttons to the material. When a color is not appropriate, place the button in a plastic bag and set aside. Explain to your class that you will use the buttons for another project. Choose two or three colors and explain that these colors will work best.

Liken the material to a lesson and buttons to ideas that will be used during the lesson (quotes, object lessons, activities, and so forth). There are many things that can be done in a lesson but we must carefully sort out the ones that work best. Other ideas, if they do not teach to the principles, should be put aside for future use.

The key to organization is simplicity. As a teacher learns and implements organizational skills, he more effectively uses time and resources. Classroom time used for teaching the gospel of Jesus Christ is a sacred trust and should be used wisely. Only those ideas that support and teach a gospel principle should be used. Organizing the lesson helps us effectively do this.

# Scripture Tools

*"I did liken all scriptures unto us, that it might be for our profit and learning."*
*—1 Nephi 19:23*

One of the greatest tools available to any teacher is the scriptures. In the scriptures the Spirit witnesses to us through the word of God, bringing to pass a change of heart. As these powerful words are understood and likened to your students' lives, great and marvelous things will transpire. As you use the scriptures in your lessons the following ideas will be helpful:

- Prayerfully select scripture passages that you will use. Make sure they reflect the objective of your lesson.
- Use pictures or other visual aids to enhance scripture stories. This will focus the students' attention and make the story more memorable.
- Have students use their scriptures to follow along as the selected verses are being read. Look up footnotes and references as a group. This will increase your students' understanding dramatically. Encourage them to mark verses that are especially meaningful to them.
- Retelling scripture stories is very effective. Read the scriptural account several times and practice telling it in your own words. This will become easier with practice.
- Role playing works well, especially with children. Remember to use simple props.
- Ask questions about the scripture stories or verses. Your questions should help students understand and apply the messages. Avoid yes or no questions. Asking who, what, when, where, why, and how can be very effective.
- Promote discussions that will help the members of your group to ponder how the scriptures apply to their individual lives. You will discover that testimonies will grow and lives will change as the scriptures are internalized.

# Music Is an Important Tool

*"Yea, the song of the righteous is a prayer unto me . . ."*
*—Doctrine and Covenants 25:12*

Music, because of its ability to bring the Spirit, can be an important addition to any lesson. Many teachers automatically dismiss the use of music in their classes because they feel uncomfortable singing. However, music is a remarkably flexible tool that can be used in many ways.

- Class singing is not always necessary. Simply listening, as a class, to an instrumental rendition can easily and effectively use a familiar hymn.
- Consider a simple reading of the words. The lyrics of any hymn are inspirational and an excellent way to include music in the lesson.
- Have your class hum while another class member quotes the lyrics.
- Have a special guest(s) come in to perform a hymn. Use solos, duets, trios, families, vocals, or instrumentals. Think about using someone from another organization, as well as someone in your own class.
- Use music to soothe, set a quiet tone, or as a change of pace within a lesson.
- Invite someone to say the words while the hymn is being played in the background. Background music can be played from a tape or as a background solo.
- Go ahead and sing! If you feel really uncomfortable, use a hymn tape as a support.